THE JESUS
CANDIDAtE

James Paul Lusk MA MPhil was born near London in 1947. Educated at Dover Grammar School and Hertford College, Oxford, he was a prizewinning Oxford University politics scholar. He has worked for the United Nations, national and local government, citizen groups, housing associations, universities, charities and co-operatives, in a career focused on improving services through community involvement and control. He has written for the national and Christian press on politics, housing and empowerment. He is active in Christian service in Kent.

THE JESUS CANDIDATE

Political religion in a secular age

James Paul Lusk

Ekklesia

First published in March 2017

Ekklesia
235 Shaftesbury Avenue
London
WC2H 8EP
www.ekklesia.co.uk

Production and design: Bob Carling (www.carling.org.uk)
Managing Editor: Simon Barrow

www.thejesuscandidate.uk

ISBN: 978-0-9932942-9-7

A Catalogue record for this book is available from the British Library.

The views in this book are not necessarily the views of the publisher.

Should Christians be aiming to 'Christianise' governments and countries through legislation? *The Jesus Candidate* examines contemporary disputes and reaches conclusions that some will find controversial. Every evangelical should read this challenging book.

Hugh Thomson, Pastor, City Evangelical Church, Birmingham

This book recasts the debate about religion, politics and the secular state. It creates the possibility of a different, more fruitful kind of conversation about how to live Christianly in a mixed-belief society.

Simon Barrow, Director of Ekklesia

Contents

Foreword

In recent years we have seen more and more Christian rhetoric directed against secularity and the liberal state in a plural society. We hear that Christianity is being 'marginalised', 'picked on', even 'persecuted' by a secular liberalism that is inherently anti-religious. These voices often also wish for the restoration of a 'Christian nation' at the level of civil and state power, on the basis that there is a biblical mandate for this and that the idea of a fair, neutral state is a myth. It must either be Christian or, effectively, anti-Christian.

In this powerful book, James Paul Lusk, writing from a socially-engaged evangelical viewpoint, seeks to show why such an attempt at reasserting Christian hegemony over a plural society is wrong theologically, flawed in its characterisation of the liberal state in relation to expressions of belief, historically ignorant of the role Christianity has played in bringing about a secular order alongside others, and deeply dangerous for all who value freedom of speech and action (whatever their religious or non-religious convictions). He considers that its British advocates owe their politics to the United States' Religious Right, prominent again in the presidency of Donald Trump.

Ekklesia has been involved in these debates for some fifteen years. We have resisted the notion that religion must either be domineering in the social order, or else entirely privatised. We have advocated civil society as the place where Christians and others can contend and collaborate for deep ethical values. We have argued on theological grounds against attempts by Christians (or anyone else) to manipulate civil and state power towards their own interests, at the expense of others – including those with whom we disagree, or find ourselves in tension. As a think tank strongly influenced by non-conformist, Anabaptist and 'peace church' traditions, we have instead pursued a vision of the church as a 'contrast society', helping to counter inequality, injustice, violence, racism and environmental destruction, both locally and globally, and witnessing to those principles in the reordering of its own life.

Contributors to Ekklesia have also argued that, far from opposing the impact of equalities legislation (discussed in detail in this book), Christians should recognise that the struggle for equality is a deeply Christian one. Seeking exemption from doing right by others contradicts the gospel of Christ, which is about a way of life based on self-giving love and neighbourly forgiveness, not coercion and antagonism. More broadly, the flourishing of our own lives depends upon creating and guarding the space in which all may flourish. So Christians can and should stand in solidarity with people of other faiths, with Humanists, agnostics and atheists, in making the case for what is now called 'universal human rights'. From a Christian perspective, such a case will be grounded in the strong conviction that 'life in all its fullness' is a gift of God and that being human therefore brings with it the inalienable qualities of dignity, sustainability, freedom and shared responsibility. Others may seek to resource their ethical commitment to mutual flourishing in different ways. This creates grounds for cooperation, discussion, debate and, yes, useful disagreement – not a cosy consensus devoid of moral challenge.

There is much in this book that is consonant with the post-Christendom perspective ('beyond the church of power') that Ekklesia is known for, but also some useful tensions. The question about whether Christian witness to the state rightly begins or ends with 'obedience' or 'submission', and whether Jesus and Paul might legitimately be read in a more radical and subversive way than happens in these pages, is one worth pursuing further, for example. But that only illustrates the fact that this book is a contribution to an ongoing conversation that we can and must take further. Its particular strength and merit, it seems to me, is that in a forthright but gracious way, it takes the argument about 'political religion in a secular age' directly to those who most fear that Christianity is being squeezed out of society by secularism, and suggests that the reverse might be the case. An open, plural, secular framework of governance, rightly understood, is not the enemy of the freedom to believe, but its friend.

One last word on the title. Though the focus of *The Jesus Candidate* is on Britain, and on mainstream Christian reasons for disavowing the political ideology of the Christian Right here, it has been impossible to ignore the fact that the later genesis of this book has been against the backdrop of Donald Trump's position as President of the United States on the other side of the Atlantic. If ever there was a warning from history about the politicisation of faith in the wrong way, the absorption of evangelical religion by aggressively reactionary ideology, and the dangers of a totalising worldview that demonises liberality and difference, the Trump campaign – heavily buttressed by Christian conservatives – is surely it. In Britain the forces of chauvinism have also been growing in recent times. In this context, faith can both liberate and imprison. Let us Christians ensure that, when it employs the the name of Christ, it does the former not the latter.

Simon Barrow
Director, Ekklesia

Author's Preface

This book is about politics and religion. It is written especially for Christians and all those interested in the changing situation in Britain. So why this book, and why now?

We are at a turning point in our history – the time when people in Britain who call themselves 'Christians' have become a social minority.[1] Meanwhile the referendum vote in favour of 'Brexit' may prompt a fundamental review of the British state and its long-standing democracy. Yet more disruptively to 'politics as usual', Donald Trump has taken the US Presidency in an election where "Catholics and white evangelicals made the difference".[2]

As things stand now, the remnants of a Christian state persist, but for practical purposes, Britain has a secular political system. This book considers three models for Christians to relate to the state in our age. One is to regard the state as properly Christian and so any alternatives are, at best, a semi-acceptable compromise. Another is to consider the state's job to be to promote the 'common good' and to work with others – 'of all faiths and of none', as the familiar saying goes – to agree on what will now make the state 'good'. This book gives reasons for rejecting each of these.

Instead it argues for the emergent Christian minority to celebrate the secular state as, in significant part, a product of New Testament thinking and of the church's struggle for its own liberty. It is time to engage to uphold a truly liberal political order based on equality between all.

This book also looks critically at the claims of the 'Religious Right'. This political movement originated in the USA in the 1970s, and its ideology is now, I suggest, being advanced in Britain by two organisations: the Christian Institute and Christian Concern. The Religious Right urges Christians to resist the secular state and instead to work to restore Christian domination in the political sphere. It uses its stories of legal cases to spread the idea that 'equality law is marginalising Christians'.

In Britain, the Religious Right is unlikely to achieve the extent of political power reached in the United States. Compared to America, Britain has fewer Christian believers, and a deep suspicion of mix-

---

1   British Social Attitudes Survey no. 30 reported that followers of all branches of Christianity comprised 46% of the British population in 2012. 6% followed other religions leaving 48% non-religious. See: www.bsa.natcen.ac.uk.

2   http://religionnews.com/2016/11/09/the-religious-factors-in-the-election/

ing religion and politics. But power and numbers are not everything. Christians are called to be 'salt and light' in society. In a democracy, all citizens take part in shaping political life. Is the Religious Right really influencing Christians to be 'salt and light' in politics – to preserve what is good in our system, and expose it to open and honest examination? My answer to that question is 'no'. This book explains why.

Some Christians say that this debate should be kept private. This is all a disagreement between Christians about matters that are 'secondary' – not the 'primary' things that divide believers and others. Sincere followers of Jesus are found on both sides of this debate. Public dispute, some say, just encourages 'secularists' who are against all religion.

I see this point of view. But the Religious Right claims to speak for Christians who have not been asked to endorse its version of radical politics. I will argue that it misrepresents Christianity as a religion of rules. It denies the Christian roots of secular politics and thus an important truth about the Christian foundation of modern society. It weakens the legitimacy of the modern state, posing risks to the orderly and capable management of complex public decisions. If it ever fully succeeds, it will menace the freedom of the church itself to control its own affairs, just as 'Christendom' did in the past. For all these reasons this debate cannot, reasonably or realistically, be properly a private matter.

Acknowledgements

My journey to writing this book started in the late 1990s, when there was talk in Baptist circles about the threats of 'pluralism' in society. Baptists think people become Christians as a mature choice, not by birth. A pluralistic society – with equal standing before the law for all, regardless of faith – follows logically from this account of Christianity. As I discussed all this with the Rev Paul Mallard, then pastor of Wood Green church in Worcester, he handed me his copy of Leonard Verduin's *The Reformers and their Stepchildren* – a history of the struggle between two views of the church. From this I learnt of the Anabaptists and those who came before them. For them, 'church' meant a free, voluntary and self-governing association of believers. Against them stood Catholic and Protestant authorities applying state power to achieve what Verduin called 'sacralism'– in which all must share one faith, by birth, not choice. My good friend the Rev John Benton, editor of the monthly *Evangelicals Now* and pastor of Chertsey Street Baptist Church in Guildford, made space in his newspaper for my Christian defence of a secular state in a pluralistic society. Don Stephens of Belvidere Road church, Liverpool, made helpful comments. The Rev Stuart Olyott asked me to do an annual lecture series on politics and pluralism for his Master's course for pastors, at what is now the Union School of Theology in south Wales. This led to invitations to speak at Christian study gatherings. Dr Digby James, of Quinta Independent Evangelical Church and Quinta Press, introduced me to Roger Williams and his great work of 1644, *The Bloudy Tenent of Persecution*. My friend and colleague Joy Squires, then chair of Worcester Labour Party and later the city's parliamentary candidate, made encouraging and thoughtful comments. *Evangelicals Now* continued to publish my reviews with a principled defence of the secular state, seeking to invite discussion on a mature, liberal Christian political consciousness. But generally in evangelical circles, the growing presence of the Religious Right tended to occupy space with its worries over gay rights, cross-wearing and the pressures causing the supposed 'marginalisation' of Christians. Then I found the Anabaptist Theology Forum (ATF), a place for biblically-informed discussion on Christian public thought. I am grateful to Stuart Murray Williams, of the Bristol Baptist College, his colleagues in the Mennonite community and the editors and writers of his 'After Christendom' book series, for their role in the Forum. After ATF heard my paper on Anabaptism, pluralism and the Religious Right, Simon Barrow of Ekklesia encouraged me to prepare this book for publication. I am most grateful to all involved in ATF, including the Rev Dr Andrew Francis, for this discussion. I am grateful to many Christians in the independent evangelical community for reading and commenting on this book as it developed. Particular thanks for detailed review and comments are due to Hugh Thomson, pastor at City Evangelical Church in Birmingham, and to Andrew Bartlett QC. Andrew and Dave Puttick, assistant minister at Emmanuel Church in Canterbury, made valuable suggestions to widen my reading. Rosemary Pepper, also of Emmanuel, offered a helpful critique. I am especially grateful to Simon Barrow and his colleagues in Ekklesia for committing to publication. I am grateful to my brothers Sean, Andy and Neil for their enthusiastic criticism and suggestions.

Above all I am deeply thankful to, and for, my wife Kay, who has patiently listened, argued and made time and space for me to persist.

Without all these, this book would be different and may not have happened at all. But none should be held responsible for the consequences. Most will disagree with at least some of what follows. In a liberal and Christian spirit, they have tried to hear what I have to say, and encouraged the work to be the best their help can make it, regardless of whether or not they share its conclusions.

Note on sources
This book draws on material in the public domain, including media reports (from on-line editions unless stated otherwise), published court judgments, books, journals and many organisations' websites, as well as the Bible. Sources are cited in footnotes. I acknowledge the valuable help of Birmingham central library, the library of the University of Kent at Canterbury, and journal access on-line through the Oxford University alumni service.

Paul Lusk
March 2017

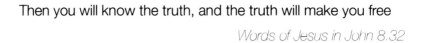

Then you will know the truth, and the truth will make you free

Words of Jesus in John 8.32

Introduction

Militant religion and secular pluralism

The rise of radical religion is a defining fact of today's politics. We see it in militant Islam, or the Religious Right in America, or local wars where groups butcher each other in the name, and perhaps the cause, of faith.

In the 1960s and 70s, when I studied politics in British universities, no one thought to prepare us for this kind of world. Democracy had defeated fascism in the Second World War, colonial empires were being dismantled, and the only challenge that mattered came from the various kinds of Marxist socialism. Then in the 1980s China and Russia turned to capitalism, and the Berlin wall, the Soviet Union and South African apartheid fell with amazing speed. It seemed that, in the words of Francis Fukuyama, "the end of history" was in view.[3] He meant that the world had reached its conclusions about the political and social solution that would endure – in the form of liberal, secular pluralism. This system advocates the maximum individual liberty consistent with a peaceful social order. It allows individuals to reach their own conclusion about what is 'good' – whether that comes from religious faith or some other set of values. Free to associate with each other, to speak and to campaign, holders of different views enjoy, at least in principle, equal rights in a 'pluralist' political setting. The system needs a powerful state to enforce order and peace, but that power is balanced by accountability to a free society and the rule of law. The state is neutral in terms of religion – it is 'secular'.

But, bubbling below the triumph of liberal pluralism, insurgent movements thought they were really responsible for the fall of Communism – and they had a different idea about the 'end of history.' The Soviets were humiliated by Afghan peasants supported not just with advanced American weapons but also by the militant Islamist worldview of the emergent al-Qaeda. In the USA, the Moral Majority plotted the rise of Ronald Reagan's Republicans. Their aim was not just to bring the Soviet Union to its knees by racking up the cost of the arms race. They wanted, in the name of 'Judaeo-Christianity,' to wage 'cultural war' against secularism. These movements – militant Islam and militant Christianity – may battle with each other. But they also have in common a battle against liberal, secular pluralism.

---

3   Francis Fukuyama, *The End of History?* The National Interest, Summer 1989. Available on-line at http://www.ou.edu/uschina/gries/articles/IntPol/Fukuyama%20End%20of%20History.pdf. Later published as a book: *The End of History and the Last Man*, Free Press, New York, 1992.

The rise and fall of Christendom

In his letter to the Romans, Paul urges Christians to confess that "Jesus Christ is Lord". But did the Apostle mean to declare Jesus 'lord' in the way we now call 'political'– as king or ruler over territory or at the head of a movement to change the control of a state? Probably not. Jesus told the authorities that his kingdom was not of (or from) this earth.[4] Satan offered supreme political power,[5] but Jesus' followers would not be "like the rulers of the gentiles, exercising authority"; rather, they were to be servants.[6] Early Christians were to live as loyal subjects of whatever political system prevailed – didn't Paul and Peter tell Christians, along with everyone else, to "be subject to the governing authorities" including "the king, as the one in authority, or to governors"?[7] Paul devoted his life to building up the Jesus movement, the *ekklesia* (church), as a multi-cultural community, but continued to identify himself as a law-abiding Jew;[8] he endured merciless persecution by all sorts of rulers, but still claimed his rights as a citizen of Rome.

And then Christianity took supreme political power in Europe. Three centuries into church history, a version of Christianity – the one approved by church authorities in Rome and Alexandria – became the official state religion of the Roman Empire. As Rome declined, this 'Christianity' moved into the empire's space at the head of an international political system – 'Christendom'. For a thousand years, churches and princes argued about who best would rule in a Christian state, and how they should rule. Christians who were able to read the New Testament sometimes questioned all this, but debating church and state authority brought punishment down on dissenters. Eventually, half way into the second millennium after Christ, printing presses flooded the market with fresh translations of the original Greek texts. It became impossible to stop the ears of Europe to the truth about the real nature of *ekklesia*. Churches could now rediscover their New Testament status as free associations of Christian believers. Once this is grasped, the political state can no longer rule with the authority of a single 'church.' So state and church became separate and distinct. Citizens were free to choose their own religious path. The state gradually ceased to claim the authority of religious truth. Christians formed independent churches, looking to the New Testament to find the way to govern themselves. Politics became 'secular.' The secular state and

---

4 John 18.36.
5 Matthew 4.8-9.
6 Matthew 20.25.
7 Romans 13.1; 1 Peter 2.13.
8 Acts 21.26.

the independent church grew in tandem, as each found it right to be free of the other's control.

In the world today, a dozen or so lands still retain a form of Christianity as their officially recognised religion. This includes the United Kingdom, where the head of state, the King or Queen, is head of the Church of England. But this feels like the charming residue of a departed age. Father Neuhaus famously complained that the 'public square' – the arena where the rights of individuals and the purposes of the democratic state are debated – is 'naked': empty of values and moral insight.[9] Equality rules, and to be a believing Christian confers no privilege in political and economic life.

Some Christians find this alarming. They fear that secular politics menaces the church, denying Christian access to the 'public square' and threatening to silence their voice. They cherish what remains of church establishment and strive for its revival.[10]

Others do not regret the loss of Christendom. They reject its under-lying claim that people become 'Christian' on the basis of their birth and political citizenship.[11] They doubt there can be such a thing as a 'Christian nation'. They may welcome the secular state.

This debate has urgent significance. For most of history, most states have submitted to a dominant religion. Is social cohesion possible in a 'pluralist' society where many different religious views have equal status? If so, how? If not, how will the struggle for control be managed and resolved?

The Religious Right and cultural war

For the last thirty years, the strongest voice of Christians alarmed at the fall of Christendom has come from the 'Religious Right'. This move-ment started in 1970s America, in the 'Moral Majority' strategy for Ronald Reagan to defeat the sitting President, the Baptist Democrat Jimmy Carter, in the 1980 election. As I seek to show in this book, in Britain its values and ideas are expressed by the Christian Institute, founded at the end of the twentieth century, and the more recently formed Christian Concern (originally called Christian Concern for Our Nation).

The roots of the Religious Right are found in the writings of two American thinkers in the Calvinist Presbyterian tradition, Roussas Rushdoony and Francis Schaeffer. Their main idea was that all law

---

9   Richard John Neuhaus, *The Naked Public Square: religion and democracy in America,* Eerdmans, Grand Rapids, 1984.
10   See for example David Holloway, *Church and State in the New Millennium,* HarperCollins, London 2000.
11   See for example Christopher Catherwood, *Whose Side is God on?: Nationalism and Christianity,* SPCK, London, 2003; Jonathan Bartley *Faith and Politics after Christendom,* Paternoster, Milton Keynes, 2006.

must have a religious basis, and the secular state is in the process of replacing biblically-based law – what they call 'Judaeo-Christian' law – with law based on anti-Christian humanism. So Christians must wage 'cultural war' against secular liberals who are said to 'hate America' and to conspire with radical Islam and Marxism to bring it down. The Religious Right's aim is for Christianity to regain the command of the social order that it has gradually lost over three centuries. To do this they must wrest control from the secular state that they denounce as an illegitimate conspiracy with America's enemies. Understanding this ideology helps explain Donald Trump's success in his campaign to be Republican candidate in the 2016 Presidential election. Mr Trump may not personally be part of the Religious Right, but its legacy provides a way to arouse grass-roots activists nourished on fear of Muslims, suspicion of anti-American conspiracy and distrust of the state. Leading Religious Right figures including Michele Bachman and James Dobson joined the Trump campaign to form a link with evangelicals.[12] Among white voters identifying themselves as 'evangelical,' four out of five backed Trump on November 8th 2016.[13]

In this book I set out reasons for rejecting the claims of the Religious Right. I will explain its political ideology, and then review some of its well-publicised legal campaigns in the UK. Some will find this analysis unduly hostile, both towards those promoting campaigns and towards sincere Christians who find themselves in court. Why not be gentler? The evidence shows that much of the publicity surrounding legal cases is misleading, even untrue. The Religious Right is, basically, a political ideology which at best is a distraction from a proper Christian evaluation of modern politics.

The case for liberalism
As the alternative to the Religious Right, I put the case for Christians to defend liberal, secular pluralism in politics. The state is a social institution with a particular function – to exercise force on behalf of society as a whole. It is for people and communities, not the state, to decide what is 'good'. In a free society, the state, with its monopoly of force, protects and empowers citizens to pursue goodness. The state is properly neutral in matters of religion. But this should not mean what some fear – excluding people of faith from the public square. A plural society promotes equality only if every set of religious values is equally wel-

---

12 http://www.donaldjtrump.com/press-releases/trump-campaign-announces-evangelical-executive-advisory-board, 21 June 2016.
13 http://www.pewforum.org/2016/07/13/evangelicals-rally-to-trump-religious-nones-back-clinton/; http://religionnews.com/2016/11/09/the-religious-factors-in-the-election/

come in that space. Society must then be able to interrogate anyone in a position of leadership and influence about how their values guide their decisions and actions. Within that framework, it is essential that Christians participate in political life. This viewpoint might be called 'substantive neutrality'.[14]

Ignorant bliss?

But is there another choice – to ignore the whole murky business of politics? The Religious Right thinks all Christians must support the cause of challenging and changing the state. I do not agree. Christians are entitled to take their own view on whether or not politics is their appropriate concern. There are many ways to be 'salt and light' in society without taking part in politics. But Christians do have a duty to submit to the state, according to the central traditions of the faith on the most straightforward reading of Romans 13.1–7. The theologian and statesman John Calvin assured most of us 450 years ago that we need not concern ourselves about politics since

> it were a very idle occupation for private men to discuss what would be the best form of polity in the place where they live, seeing these deliberations cannot have any influence in determining any public matter.[15]

Then, only a small elite had any business with politics. But now, in a modern democracy, all have "influence in determining any public matter". Christians share with other citizens in deciding "the best form of polity". Accepting this responsibility is part of what it now means to give proper recognition to the state. Christianity has shaped the modern state through a thousand and more years of 'Christendom', then in the complex unwinding of the church-state system. Christians should be able to help society understand how it came to be where it is, and how to learn from this past. So while I acknowledge the right of Christians and others to ignore politics, I think it is necessary for some to give time and attention to the place of faith and church in the public square.

Outline of the book

The first chapter starts with the words that give the book its title. Every four years, Americans elect their President. Rick Santorum, a devout Catholic, campaigned to be the Republican candidate in 2012. We see him telling a meeting that 'every election needs a Jesus candidate' –

---

14 Rex Ahdar and Ian Leigh, *Religious Freedom in the Liberal State,* OUP, Oxford, 2005, p89.
15 John Calvin, 'Of civil government', ch 20 in *Institutes of the Christian Religion,* para 8. http://www.ccel.org/ccel/calvin/institutes/

even if he or she is 'not necessarily a Christian'. What did he mean? The answer is found by examining the 'Religious Right' and its mission to rebuild a Christian state based on 'Judaeo-Christian' law.

The British arm of this mission focuses on trying to show that the law is biased against Christians. Chapter 2 considers court and media reports of some cases. Distorted and even untrue reports appear in the media, supporting the claim that Christians are 'marginalised by equality law'. Christians do sometimes face real attacks on freedom of speech, and suffer as a result, but the ordinary law applying equally to all citizens is sufficient to provide redress.

Chapter 3 considers the centuries-old debates between Christians over the proper relationship between church and state. The Religious Right looks back to two moments in history when Christianity achieved the status of a public faith. The first was after 380AD, when Catholic Christianity was established as the state religion of the Roman Empire. The second came on the American continent, in Calvinist Protestant control over the colony of Massachusetts in New England from the 1630s. After 1642, civil wars in the British islands became a struggle between different visions for the future of church and state – a struggle with a transatlantic dimension as ideas and people flowed between England and its American colonies. Some Christians seeking freedom of conscience developed the idea of separating the two – the vision later realised in the United States of America, where the church flourished after separation from the state. But recently, continuing growth of the 'hedge' between faith and state has raised fears of a moral and spiritual vacuum in politics and what might fill it.

Chapter 4 seeks to resolve this question in terms that uphold the classic Baptist case for the independence of the church. Christians, I argue, should support and defend a genuinely secular state based on equality before the law. To be truly plural and neutral in matters of faith, the state must be open to the full range of faith perspectives and the values they bring. But the state is there to serve the public purpose of security and burden-sharing, not to do the bidding of any particular moral or religious perspective. Faith cannot be a 'private' matter for a public servant. Rather her values are to be open to interrogation as part of her accountability for performing the proper functions for which the state exists – no less, and no more.

This is where emperors worshipped the God of Land and the God of Grain

From a sign at Zhongshan Park, Beijing,
Peoples Republic of China

Chapter 1

'Every election needs a Jesus candidate'

Primary question

It is 5th January 2012, in Windham, New Hampshire, USA.

Six feet and four inches tall, Rick Santorum stands before six hundred people in a school hall. Republicans are closing in on their choice of candidate for President. State by state, territory by territory, party supporters vote in primary elections for their man or woman to enter the contest against sitting President Barack Obama. Republicans in Iowa have just met and given Mr Santorum 25% of their support, putting him equal first with the Mormon businessman Mitt Romney. In a few days, on Tuesday January 10th, Republican supporters here in New Hampshire will vote in their primary election.

Mr Santorum, a devout Roman Catholic, now has the opportunity to be the voice for the 'Religious Right'. Previously, there was Michelle Bachman, accused of saying how much better African American family life used to be, under slavery;[16] sixth in Iowa, she has abandoned her campaign. There was Rick Perry, governor of Texas, opening his campaign with a prayer meeting and a video affirming that he is 'Not Ashamed' of being a Christian, but later unable to remember, in a live TV debate, which three federal Government departments he pledges to abolish. After coming fifth in Iowa, his campaign is faltering. Still in the race, fourth in Iowa with half of Mr Santorum's support, is Newt Gingrich, another Catholic, promising an American colony on the Moon.[17]

In Windham, the meeting has been going on for two hours, the chair has called time and people are starting to leave. But Mr Santorum says he will take two more questions. Someone puts one, but the candidate does not answer it. There is something else on his mind. Earlier that day, he says, a radio interviewer challenged him with these words from a listener: "We don't need a Jesus candidate – we need an economic candidate". Rick shifts his head slightly to one side and raises his eyebrows, acknowledging the wit of the challenge – and preparing

---

16 http://www.forbes.com/sites/oshadavidson/2011/07/08/michele-bachmann-salutes-the-upside-to-slavery/
17 http://www.forbes.com/sites/erikkain/2012/01/28/why-newt-gingrichs-moon-colony-is-a-good-idea-and-why-its-still-not-possible/

the audience to enjoy his counter-blow. There are a few claps. People about to leave the room stop to turn their eyes back to the tall, engaging figure who has held their attention for this evening.

> And my answer to that was: 'We always need...'

– a pause; the room falls silent –

> 'a Jesus candidate!'

Prolonged whooping and clapping break out. But Mr Santorum has something to add. Holding up his hand to restore calm, he continues:

> Now I don't mean by that that we need a Jesus candidate, someone who's a Christian, but we need someone who believes in something more than themselves – some higher power, some god, and not just the economy.[18]

In the vote on 10th January, Mr Santorum comes fourth with 9% of the vote, fractionally ahead of his rival Newt Gingrich. Neither of them leads even one of the 234 local neighbourhood votes that feed into the state-wide result. But this primary is never going to settle the question of the Religious Right's candidate. New Hampshire lies in the USA's liberal north east, far from the southern Bible belt where such matters are determined. So why use a school hall in Windham to appeal for votes for a "Jesus candidate", for the believer in "some god"?

The real award is not to be won here in New Hampshire. Mr Santorum has his eyes on another vote, involving 150 leaders meeting in a judge's private ranch outside Houston, Texas. Here on Saturday 14th January, Tony Perkins, head of the Family Research Council (FRC), announces that the conference has endorsed Mr Santorum's candidacy. Forty years old, the FRC is the most durable of the organisations founded by evangelical ministers in the aftermath of the Religious Right's victorious rising against their fellow Christian, President Jimmy Carter. Then a new movement called the Moral Majority helped deny Carter a second term and elect Ronald Reagan in his place in 1980. Now in 2012, the FRC's backing confirms Rick Santorum as the best approximation to an official Jesus candidate.

Get out of America!

A few weeks later, at the Sunday evening service in the church in Louisiana where Mr Perkins is a member, the Senior Pastor of Greenwell Springs Baptist church (motto: *the Fellowship of Excitement*), welcomes Rick Santorum to the service. The congregation stands clapping and cheering as Pastor Dennis Terry proclaims:

---

18 Video on http://www.rawstory.com/rs/2012/01/06/santorum-americans-need-a-jesus-candidate/

This nation was founded as a Christian nation – the God of Abraham, the God of Isaac and the God of Jacob – there's only one God! There's only one God and his name is Jesus! I'm tired of people telling me that I can't say those words. I'm tired of people telling us as Christians that we can't voice our beliefs or we can no longer pray in public. Listen to me, If you don't love America, If you don't like the way we do things I have one thing to say – GET OUT! We don't worship Buddha! I say we don't worship Buddha, we don't worship Mohammad, we don't worship Allah, we worship God, we worship God's son Jesus Christ.

Christianity, he says, "is the key to the economy turning round, to bringing the jobless rate down – it's a spiritual thing". Then Rick Santorum submits as the Southern Baptist minister reaches up an arm, nearly managing to reach the top of the tall Catholic's bowed head, and prays for God to favour his candidacy.[19]

A storm breaks over the head of Pastor Terry as the video of the 'GET OUT' sermon goes viral, showing up on tens of thousands of websites across the world. Nervous in the unaccustomed limelight, the Pastor insists that he does not hate non-Christians. Has he told them to get out of America? No, his defenders say. The Pastor has defended freedom of religion. As the Rightscoop website put it on March 12th, what Pastor Terry meant was

We're Christians and we have a right to say it, a right to pray it, and you don't have the right to take that away from us. If you don't like freedom of religion, if you don't like freedom of speech, if you don't like our Constitution, if you don't like the way we do things in America, GET OUT![20]

So it is those "telling us Christians that we can't voice our beliefs" who should "get out". Rick Santorum says that he did not applaud this part of the sermon.

After winning primaries in 11 of the 32 states to have voted so far, Santorum ends his bid for the Presidency on Tuesday 10th April, making way for the Religious Right to give its reluctant support to Mitt Romney. As Americans go to the national polls in November, Pastor Terry announces that he has answered God's call to leave his ministry in Louisiana and move immediately to a small work, newly established by Southern Baptist missionaries, in Trinity, Alabama, along state Highway 24 some 20 miles east of Huntsville. Pastor Terry's first sermon at Family Baptist church (*'our goal is to encourage and equip parents to succeed in the God given task of discipling their children in their homes'*) is a message for New Year 2013. His next sermon is entitled 'courageous leadership.'

---

19 A video of all this is widely available on the internet, see for example: http://www.huffingtonpost.com/2012/03/19/dennis-terry-rick-santorum_n_1364414.html

20 http://therightscoop.com/stop-taking-pastor-dennis-terry-out-of-context-he-said-nothing-wrong/

What the Religious Right believes

What are we to make of all this? Rick Santorum asserts that "every election needs a Jesus candidate". Does Jesus Christ call on his followers to put themselves forward, in his name, as candidates for offices of state? Should positions in government and Congress or Parliament – positions as rulers and law-makers – be taken in his name or on his behalf?

In the New Testament, two people suggest that Jesus might be this kind of political and legal ruler. The first is Satan, who offers a deal: follow me, abandon God, and take over every kingdom around – which Jesus rejects.[21] The second is Pontius Pilate, who after sentencing Jesus to death, puts 'King of the Jews' on the charge sheet at the execution site.[22]

Jesus himself tells Pilate[23] that his kingdom is "not from this earth". In the New Testament, soldiers and tax-collectors – vital agents in the rule of pagan Rome – are told that the requirement on them, as members of this kingdom, is to do their jobs honestly and honourably.[24] When Caesar demands taxes, pay up – it is, after all, his face on the money.[25] So if being the 'Jesus Candidate' means someone who seeks political office in the name of Jesus, this may be to move away from Christ's teaching as recorded in the Bible, at least according to majority evangelical understandings.

But Rick Santorum is not making this claim. He goes on to say that the 'Jesus candidate' is "not someone who's a Christian, but ... someone who believes in something more than themselves – some higher power, some god". Some god – *any* god? *Anyone* with faith "in something more than themselves"? Could this definition cover a follower of, say, Osama bin Laden or Karl Marx – could either of these be the 'Jesus candidate' against someone who offers a programme based on "just the economy"? The surprising answer to this question is 'yes' and to understand the thinking here, it is necessary to penetrate the philosophy of the 'Religious Right'. This movement is founded on the idea that the work of shaping and enforcing the law – the work of the 'state' – is *necessarily* religious. It is not possible for things to be any other way. In the words of the founder of Christian Reconstructionism, Roussas J. Rushdoony:

---

21 Matthew 4.8–9.
22 John 19.19.
23 John 18.36.
24 Luke 3.12–15.
25 Mark 12.16–17.

Law is in every culture *religious in origin*.[26] Because law governs man and society, because it establishes and declares the meaning of justice and righteousness, law is inescapably religious, in that it establishes the ultimate concerns of a culture ... no disestablishment of religion as such is possible in any society ... No society exists without a religious foundation or without a law-system which codifies the morality of its religion.[27]

According to Rushdoony, religious tolerance – that is to say, a pluralistic society with civil equality between those of different faiths – is impossible. "Toleration is a device used to introduce a new law-system as a prelude to a new intolerance." All states are necessarily hostile to Christianity as they establish their own law-system which is, by definition, an alternative religion. So all politics is evil. In time, according to Rushdoony, the rotten state system will die and Christians will rule over free communities governed under the Mosaic law of the Old Testament – including execution for 18 crimes, to be carried out by the 'congregation.' But meanwhile, among political movements and parties, conservatives "being less advanced and less systematic, represent the statist evil in milder form".[28] Political action can create zones of self-government for Christian communities, for instance in the sphere of family life and education. Free market economics is a means to realise the vision of a stateless society in keeping with the natural harmony that God wills.

From the 1960s to the 1980s, Rushdoony worked with diligence, as well as with money from business foundations, to build a following in churches and far-right networks. His disciple and son-in-law Gary North developed 'Christian Economics' as an ultra-free-market system for society to function without the state, and worked assisting Ron Paul, then the most prominent politician on the libertarian wing of American politics (a role since taken by his son Rand Paul). So Rushdoony's theory of 'Theonomy' (the rule of God's law) went hand in hand with the revival of free-market economics, and built an alliance with the rising 'libertarian' pro-market strand on the American right.

Rushdoony was admired as an intellectual and visionary and taken seriously among mainstream evangelicals as a political theologian. His influence in building the new Religious Right is only now being understood.[29] But Rushdoony dismissed democracy and tolerance. He was a holocaust denier, commenting that the number of Jews killed by Nazi

---

26 Original italics.
27 R. J. Rushdoony *Institutes of biblical law,* Presbyterian and Reformed Publishing Co, 1973: pp4–5.
28 R J Rushdoony, *Christianity and the state,* Kindle edition, Loc 488.
29 Michael J. McVicar, *Christian Reconstruction: R.J. Rushdoony and American Religious Conservatism,* University of North Carolina Press, Chapel Hill, 2015.

persecution was grossly exaggerated (in what he saw as a case of "false testimony" as denounced by the Ninth Commandment) and that the allied bombing of Germany was a crime on an equivalent scale. All this made Rushdoony too extreme to be the public face of the movement.

The Reconstructionist positions on the religious basis of state, law and culture were adopted and popularised by a much more visible figure: Francis Schaeffer, who became the 'intellectual father' of the American Religious Right.[30] Led by its founder Jerry Falwell, and enthusiastically applauded by Schaeffer, the Moral Majority took grass-roots control of the Republican Party as part of its deal with Ronald Reagan at the end of the 1970s.[31] Asked to name the thinkers who most influenced them, leaders of the Religious Right from Jerry Falwell[32] through to Michelle Bachman[33] have consistently named Schaeffer. Katherine Harris, who as secretary of state for Florida played a key role in delivering the presidency to George W Bush in the 2000 election, was a disciple of Schaeffer.[34]

A philosophy graduate, Presbyterian minister and missionary to Europe, Schaeffer and his family ran a retreat in the Swiss mountains from where he established an extraordinary reputation as an evangelical polymath, especially through a book entitled *How Should We Then Live?* Schaeffer expounded a panoramic view of culture, the arts, science, philosophy and history, in which Christianity is not just 'truth' but 'true truth' – the God-given framework within which all knowledge is validated, and without which all enquiry is a power-struggle between competing relativisms. The book was linked to a film series, expensively produced with Catholic funding,[35] where Schaeffer appears in mountain-style knickerbockers tucked into knee-high socks, his flowing hair swept back onto his shoulders, and a long grey goatee-style beard, expounding his views on art, science and law. In 1982 he was hailed by *Newsweek* magazine as the 'guru of fundamentalism.' This singular individual's lofty Christian philosophy subordinated all knowledge and experience within one overarching idea, easily digested in moving pictures. After the trauma of the Kennedy assassination,

30 D G Hart, *From Billy Graham to Sarah Palin: Evangelicals and the Betrayal of American Conservatism*, Eerdmans, Grand Rapids, 2011, p76.

31 There are many texts on the history of the links built between the Republican Party and the Religious Right. See for example D G Hart (above), chapter 4 and Craig Unger (below) chapter 2.

32 Speaking to a Baptist convention on 26th October 2004, Falwell testified to Schaeffer's influence: "Back in the '50s, '60s, and '70s, of my generation he was the guru of all the evangelicals" – and explained how in meetings from the 1960s onwards, Schaeffer challenged him to engage in cultural and political issues (Article on bpnews.net, posted 29 October 2004, by Jerry Pierce).

33 Ryan Lizza, 'Leap of Faith' – a profile of a Republican front-runner posted on *New Yorker* website, 15th August 2011.

34 Craig Unger, *The Fall of the House of Bush*, Simon and Schuster, London, 2007, p177.

35 Interview with the producer of the series, Francis Schaeffer's son Frank, http://www.pbs.org/godinamerica/interviews/frank-schaeffer.html

the Vietnam war, race riots and the criminality of the Nixon presidency, this 'guru' seemed to offer a way to bring alienated young people back into the fold of Christian America.

Schaeffer's political thinking was expounded in *How Should We Then Live?* and consolidated in *A Christian Manifesto*, published in 1981. He acknowledges as his main influence the Scottish Presbyterian theologian and legal theorist Samuel Rutherford, who died in 1661 before his major work, *Lex Rex* (the Law is King) was published. Schaeffer explains that the USA was founded as a Christian country with a 'Judaeo-Christian' system of law based on the Old and New Testament Scriptures. With the state understood to be subordinate to the law, which was in turn subordinate to God's provision of justice, personal liberty was guaranteed by the limited power of the state.

Schaeffer concedes that most individuals are not believing and worshipping Christians. Nonetheless, he says, the social system still carries a memory of Christian legal provision. But the twentieth century saw this religious dominance challenged by secular humanism. This denies there is a creator-God, sees existence as a product of material chance, and allows humanity to determine its own law in the interests of those most equipped to impose their will. This leads to what Schaeffer calls 'sociological law' produced by a small elite group that decides for itself what is best for society (i.e., in practice, for themselves). With no religious authority conferring protection on the weak, the result is law based on power and self-interest. Abortion – legalised in the USA by the Supreme Court in 1973, using an interpretation of the constitutional right to privacy – was a manifestation of such man-made law, with its disrespect for the God-given rights of individuals and the moral conscience of the majority. Without religious authority, the state commands no voluntary assent, and rules only by force. The secular state, with a plurality of views apparently given equal status, represents a world view which is totally opposed to, and must seek to destroy, Christianity. Politicians and law courts are the instruments of this attack. Disagreeing with Rushdoony (and with Rutherford), Schaeffer held that freedom and personal choice in religious matters *are* possible, but only under the protection of a supreme God-based legality. Once this is removed, freedom inevitably comes under attack. Humanism is an alternative religion, and Christians must work before it is too late to expose the Humanist, materialist law system for the anti-human conspiracy that it really is. This can be done through legal challenge, democratic organisation and active disobedience to the state, including action to expose and prevent immoral actions (such as abortion) promoted by the state. The Moral Majority, or something like it, is essential to:

> use the freedom we still have in the political arena to stand against the other total entity ... all Christians have got to do the same kind of thing or you are simply not showing the Lordship of Christ in the totality of life[36]

The 1980 American presidential election, and its 'conservative swing' (to Reagan) allowed the opening of a 'unique window' for Christians to 'roll back the other total entity'.[37] The task for Christians in the 'window' is to:

> take the steps necessary to break the authoritarian hold which the material-energy, chance concept of final reality has on government and law[38]

All Christians must be prepared for active disobedience against the state – otherwise they are not 'living under the Scripture'.[39]

Knowing the political outlook of the Religious Right helps us to understand Pastor Terry's 'Get out!' sermon. He said America is a Jesus-worshipping country – those not ready to accept this should 'Get out'. Waves of indignation flooded in – was the pastor, and the Religious Right, denying religious freedom? No, said Pastor Terry's (and Rick Santorum's) defenders. The people being told to 'Get out' were those wanting to restrict the freedom of Christians to express their faith. So was the pastor arguing for political authority to rest with followers of Jesus, or was he arguing for freedom for Christians to be themselves? To his critics, there was an obvious distinction between these two positions. However, this is not a difference that Pastor Terry, or Tony Perkins, or Rick Santorum, from their perspective, would see as significant. For them, the political system is necessarily religious. The best, maybe only, way to secure the liberty of Christians *and* of those of other faiths is to base law and political authority on the Judaeo-Christian tradition. Those who claim authority in the name of other 'gods' may be hostile to Christianity, but at least they have the merit of being honest about the religious character of their politics – in Rick Santorum's words, at least they follow "some god" and not "just the economy". Worse are those who think the state can be neutral in such matters – supposing that it is possible for the state to operate without any religious allegiance. According to Rushdoony and Schaeffer and the Religious Right, the secular state is a cover for nihilism and an as-

---

36 *Manifesto*, pp.61/2.
37 Page 73/4.
38 Page 136.
39 Page 134.

sault on Christianity. Pastor Terry's sermon simply reiterates this: religious liberty is possible in a system that sees Jesus-worship as the foundation of its political and legal existence; those who want some other terms are denying liberty to Christians and to others; if they do not wish to live in the USA on these terms they should live somewhere else.

Rick Santorum was widely derided for what he made of a famous speech made by John F Kennedy as a candidate for the Presidency in 1960. Kennedy became the first, and so far only, Roman Catholic President. He wanted to assure the Protestant majority that he would not rule as the agent of the Vatican. Kennedy's definitive response to these fears was to declare his commitment to a secular political system:

> I believe in an America where the separation of church and state is absolute, where no Catholic prelate would tell the president (should he be Catholic) how to act, and no Protestant minister would tell his parishioners for whom to vote; where no church or church school is granted any public funds or political preference; and where no man is denied public office merely because his religion differs from the president who might appoint him or the people who might elect him.

> I believe in an America that is officially neither Catholic, Protestant nor Jewish; where no public official either requests or accepts instructions on public policy from the Pope, the National Council of Churches or any other ecclesiastical source; where no religious body seeks to impose its will directly or indirectly upon the general populace or the public acts of its officials; and where religious liberty is so indivisible that an act against one church is treated as an act against all.

> For while this year it may be a Catholic against whom the finger of suspicion is pointed, in other years it has been, and may someday be again, a Jew – or a Quaker or a Unitarian or a Baptist. It was Virginia's harassment of Baptist preachers, for example, that helped lead to Jefferson's statute of religious freedom. Today I may be the victim, but tomorrow it may be you – until the whole fabric of our harmonious society is ripped at a time of great national peril.

> Finally, I believe in an America where religious intolerance will someday end; where all men and all churches are treated as equal; where every man has the same right to attend or not attend the church of his choice; where there is no Catholic vote, no anti-Catholic vote, no bloc voting of any kind; and where Catholics, Protestants and Jews, at both the lay and pastoral level, will refrain from those attitudes of disdain and division which have so often marred their works in the past, and promote instead the American ideal of brotherhood.[40]

Rick Santorum said that, when he read these words from Kennedy, he wanted to "throw up".

---

40   Speech by J F Kennedy to the Greater Houston Ministerial Association, 12th September 1960. Full transcript on: http://www.npr.org/templates/story/story.php?storyId=16920600

To say that people of faith have no role in the public square? You bet that makes you throw up ... What kind of country do we live in that says only people of non-faith can come into the public square and make their case?'[41]

Many commentators thought that Santorum was 'confused' and had misunderstood Kennedy as suggesting that people of faith should not enter political discussion. But on the logic of the Religious Right, Santorum's analysis is correct. Governing and law-making are, in this view, necessarily religious actions. If religious frames of reference, and obedience to religious authority, are not the basis of participation, then people with an explicit religious faith are excluded. Only those without faith can enter; and theirs is in fact an alternative religion, that of secular Humanism. A day or two later Santorum expressed regret for the reference to vomiting, but went on to say Kennedy's views "triggered in my opinion the privatisation of faith and I think that's a bad thing".[42]

It may come as a surprise that the separation of church and state, as endorsed by President Kennedy, should be considered controversial. It is widely assumed that the American constitution guarantees this separation, through the first amendment passed in 1791 whereby "Congress shall make no law respecting an establishment of religion". However, this was a *federal* law. The USA is a federation of states – there were 14 states when the Bill of Rights, including the first amendment, was ratified. The point of the first amendment was to stop the federal government imposing or establishing a religion, but states could – and did – continue to have their own established religions. From 1861 to 1865, Americans fought a Civil War over the power of the federal regime to direct the internal affairs of the states. The fourteenth amendment, made after the war, prevented local government from depriving citizens of life, liberty or property without due process. In the twentieth century the federal courts used this 'due process clause' to extend the protections of the Bill of Rights to all government decisions. Here is an important source of aggravation for the Religious Right. They see the abandonment of Judaeo-Christian law, and its replacement with 'sociological' law, as the main key to understanding the anti-Christian, anti-religious nature of the secular state as it emerged in the twentieth century. It is a central part of what Santorum calls the 'privatisation' of faith. And, they claim, this law was not made democratically by elected politicians, but by the courts with their secularist agenda![43]

---

41   ABC news report, 26 February 2013: http://abcnews.go.com/blogs/politics/2012/02/rick-santorum-jfks-1960-speech-made-me-want-to-throw-up/

42   http://thinkprogress.org/lgbt/2012/02/28/433696/santorum-backs-away-from-jfk-throw-up-remark-i-wish-i-had-that-particular-line-back/

43   See for example Rushdoony *Christianity and the State:* "all the states had their own religious establishments ... Only after the Supreme Court interpreted the Fourteenth amendment to apply to all states was there a denial of the power of the states to make such establishments." In fact the usual assessment is that Massachusetts in 1834 was the last state to

One reason *every election needs a Jesus candidate* is in order to roll back the slide towards secular humanism as the official doctrine of the public sphere, and restore the place of religion at the centre of law, government and politics.

The British Religious Right

The Rev David Holloway is the parish Vicar of the Church of England in Jesmond, a suburb of Newcastle-upon-Tyne. He was among the founders, and remains a trustee, of the Christian Institute, which campaigns for greater Christian influence in politics in Britain. The Rev Holloway wrote:

> When the church fails to influence society and its rules and regulations so that they conform as much as possible to God's will, the result is not happy neutrality. Rather the result is a nasty 'spiritual and psychological slum'.[44]

For Holloway "the big issues for public life are no longer 'political' but 'cultural'". Humanists "make the State their Church" so all political action is in fact religious – "the foundations of law are inescapably religious" so any change in the political order is a change of religion. This is "culture war" – the war being "waged for the soul of the west". Elections, campaigns and legal actions are manoeuvres in this wider war. Christianity may co-exist with other faiths in a plural society, but only from a position of dominance over culture and law, a dominance which will ensure an adequately compliant political life. If society stops submitting to the Christian world view – the Judaeo-Christian evaluation of law, art and society – then freedom, truth and order will all fail as Christianity itself is extinguished. These are the stakes in the cultural war. The political analysis passed down from Rushdoony and Schaeffer is clearly present here. As the Christian Institute explains in its policy statement on church and state:

> No state can be neutral in terms of morality or religion ... To fail to privilege one religion would be for the State positively to endorse either a secular humanistic philosophy (which results in atheism), or a "multifaith philosophy".[45]

The Rev Holloway wants us to consider the relationship between 'church' and 'state' and for this purpose the 'church' includes not just 'Christian believers' but also the 'well-wishers' who:

---

scrap its legal establishment of a Christian denomination, well before the fourteenth amendment. In Everson v Board of Education (1947), the Supreme Court considered a claim over public funding of student travel to a Catholic School, and ruled that the 'wall of separation' banned any state support of religious activity. "No tax ... can be levied to support any religious activities or institutions ... whatever form they may adopt to teach or practice religion."

44 David Holloway, *Church and state in the new millennium*, London, HarperCollins, 2000, p2.

45 http://www.christian.org.uk/who-we-are/what-we-believe/christianity-and-the-state/

prefer the way of Christ to the way that leads to the spiritual slums. They often appear in the opinion polls as 'Christian' but not as regular churchgoers.

He defines the state as:

human society united both geographically and under a system of enforceable rules and regulations.

To stay out of the spiritual slum, the Church's mission, he says, is to:

influence society and its rules and regulations so that they conform as much as possible to God's will.

The meaning of this could not be clearer. As a political organisation, the church exists to enforce God's will through rule-making. This is the wish of people who 'prefer' things that way, and tell 'opinion polls' that they are Christians, even though they lack faith and do not take part in church business. Since these are not 'regular churchgoers', this leaves people who actually participate in the church to take charge of its political mission. Those who follow Christ must be persuaded to turn their time and energy to the business of public rule-making.

A study of the British Religious Right by the Theos think tank[46] found:

co-ordination among Christian groups with a strong socially-conservative commitment, in particular relating to human sexuality, marriage, family life, and religious freedom, about which they are vocal and often willing to resort to legal action. This is a familiar picture within US politics[47]

The most significant parts of this network are the Christian Institute (CI) and Christian Concern (CC) (originally founded under the name Christian Concern for our Nation). Theos says that these two organisations – CI and CC – have a close relationship with two prominent national newspapers, the *Daily Mail* and *Daily Telegraph,* so they attract exceptional amounts of publicity for legal cases they bring for alleged discrimination against Christians. Christian Concern, working with the American organisation the Alliance Defense Fund (renamed Alliance Defending Freedom in 2012), has established the Wilberforce Academy which aims to recruit able young Christian students to work on developing a policy agenda. The Director of the Wilberforce Academy is Dr Joseph Boot, a British pastor based in Toronto and active in a number

46 Part of the British and Foreign Bible Society.
47 Andy Walton with Andrea Hatcher and Nick Spencer: *Is there a 'religious right' emerging in Britain?* Theos, London, 2013, p8;,p54. Their full list of British 'Religious Right' organisations was: CARE (Christian Action and Research – originally the 1971 Festival of Light); Christian Institute (founded in 1990); Christian Concern and its Christian Legal Centre (formed 2004 out of a breakaway group from the Christian Lawyers' Fellowship); Christian Voice (set up in 1994, with a fully Reconstructionist agenda and run by Stephen Green); Christian Peoples Alliance and Christian Party (originating in the 1990s and operating mainly in east London where it has had councillors elected); Conservative Christian Fellowship (focused on a number of MPs); and Evangelical Alliance (a mainstream evangelical body with roots in the mid-19th century).

of Californian ministries as well as in ADF. Dr Boot expects Christians to "take back powers over education, medicine, charity, welfare, the state" and act politically to "vote for leaders who will establish true worship". According to Dr Boot, the retreat from political power after the Reformation is a main cause of the decline of Christianity in the West, as "the state that acknowledges God's law becomes the nursery of Christianity". Dr Boot wants a return to a formally Christian state: he does not "believe that our forebears got it wrong for 1500 years".[48] The CC website features 35 of Dr Boot's videos, with articles including favourable references to Rushdoony and his followers.

The launch of the Wilberforce Academy was linked to a Christian Concern campaign called *Not Ashamed*. The campaign invited Christian believers to wear the 'Not Ashamed' logo and slogans on t-shirts and wristbands. On the campaign website, Lord Carey, the former Archbishop of Canterbury, complained that "the Christian Faith is in danger of being stealthily and subtly brushed aside". His book, co-written with his son, accused the "militant wing of secularism" of mounting a "crusade" aiming "to eradicate religion in general – and Christianity in particular – from any role in public life". A "few brave Christian souls have had the courage to stand up against bullying tactics and, as a result, lost employment … for to hold to principles central to biblical Christianity is now being increasingly seen as unacceptable".[49] Corrupted by secularism, the law courts are "trespassing on matters that belong to the realm of theology".[50] Lord Carey urged senior judges to "recuse" (exclude) themselves from considering cases where they lacked the qualification to understand religious issues. Instead he suggested that special panels of religiously-qualified judges would consider all cases, affecting all faiths, where religion formed part of the defence. Not surprisingly, the Justices declined to sack themselves, using words Lord Carey found "withering and scornful".[51]

The guiding mind behind Christian Concern (CC) is its chief executive Andrea Minichiello Williams, a barrister who describes herself as a 'missionary lawyer' whose "heart cries out for a lost and broken nation that has turned her back on the truth of the gospel". She sees CC as a means to provide the "legal and policy expertise needed to campaign against the secularisation and islamisation of Great Britain".[52] In tak-

---

48 In an event hosted by Christian Concern, entitled 'open forum on contemporary culture'. A video is on http://www.
    christianconcern.com/search/node/Gospel%20Truth%20in%20Contemporary%20Culture%20open%20forum
49 George and Andrew Carey, *We don't do God: the marginalisation of public faith*, Oxford: Monarch, 2012, pp 9–10.
50 p100.
51 Lord Carey's intervention in the Macfarlane case and the judicial response are considered further in the next chapter.
52 Interview in *Evangelicals Now*, April 2009.

ing legal actions through the European Court of Human Rights, CC has been supported by the Alliance Defending Freedom, which has placed its own lawyers on the legal teams.[53]

British thinking behind the Christian Institute and Christian Concern – represented in the writings of the Rev David Holloway and Lord Carey – shares much with the American Religious Right. Central to this is the idea, inherited from Rushdoony and Schaeffer, that the religious foundation of the legal system has been eroded and that its secular replacement is anti-Christian in sentiment and judgement. Legal action tries to tackle the injustices that result from discrimination – but also provides a platform to attack the courts and discredit the judiciary in the eyes of Christians.

Bibles and tablets of stone

Outside Northern Ireland, religious candidates are rarely seen in elections in the United Kingdom, and a contender presenting him or herself as the 'Jesus candidate' would be greeted with gales of laughter.

But this does not mean that religion has no place in the concerns of the main political parties. At the end of 2011, David Cameron, then the British Prime Minister, spoke at an event in Westminster Abbey, London, to mark the 400th anniversary of the publication of the 'authorised' King James Version of the Bible in English. "Britain is a Christian country" he said. "And we should not be afraid to say so." He described himself as a "committed" but "vaguely practising Church of England Christian" who would "stand up for the values and principles" of this faith.

A few months later, every secondary school in the land received a package. Inside was one copy of the King James Bible, the translation made four centuries ago, with a cover reading:

> **The Holy Bible. Quatercentenary edition.**
> **Presented by the secretary of state for education.**

Michael Gove, who was that secretary of state, explained that this was sent because "pupils should learn about its role in the nation's history, language, literacy and culture". The cost – £377,000 – was met not by his department but by private sources, some known as donors to the Conservative party, topped up with £91,000 from the Bible Society.[54] In a radio interview, Mr Gove said he did not authorise the

---

53 There is more on this in the next chapter, 'Court in the act'.
54 The Bible Society's accounts for the year ending in 2013 included one grant of £91,000 paid to the Department for Education for the 'KJV project.' For reported other donors, see: http://www.theguardian.com/politics/2012/may/15/michael-gove-king-james-bible

inscription 'presented by the secretary of state for education' and did not even know about it until seeing the first copy.[55]

Later in 2012, the then leader of the British Labour Party, Ed Miliband, gave his annual leader's speech to the party conference. The speech was noted for its attempt to launch Labour as the party of "One Nation" – a term used 47 times. He also spoke about his "faith" – using that word twelve times. An atheist, Ed Miliband nonetheless claimed to have a "faith that many religious people would recognise". A key influence on the thinking in this speech here is a movement called 'Blue Labour.' This came out of a body of theological thought calling itself Radical Orthodoxy, developed by Professor John Milbank. It teaches that liberalism and secularism have run their course and we are moving into a 'post liberal' world where only a 'theological vision' can effectively both understand and devise an alternative to 'liberalism'. This vision is to restore a relational, personal and trust-based society, a more democratic version of what Professor Milbank sees in the great virtues of pre-Reformation Catholic communities. Another significant presence in the Radical Orthodoxy movement is Phillip Blond, formerly an academic theologian. He is a Conservative known to have influenced David Cameron's 'Big Society' theme, especially through his book *Red Tory*,[56] and is founder of a political think-tank called Respublica. Blond is personally very close to Maurice, now Lord, Glasman, once a close advisor to Ed Miliband and the most public face of Blue Labour.[57] For Radical Orthodoxy, left and right are "secular categories" inherited from the French Revolution. The movement aims to "rebaptise civil society". A renewed covenant with God is the only rescue from liberal capitalism.[58] A few days before the 2015 General Election, Ed Miliband stunned his party by producing a limestone tablet, eight feet and six inches high, on which were carved his six election promises with his signature at the end. This tablet, he said, would be erected outside his official residence in Downing Street should he become Prime Minister. The atheist Labour leader's reference to himself as Moses was unmissable.

Radical Orthodoxy does not share the Religious Right's preoccupation with law. It is more at home on the centre and left of politics

---

55 In an interview on BBC World at One May 2012. https://audioboom.com/boos/818668-michael-gove-on-teacher-morale-curriculum-changes-and-sending-bibles-to-schools

56 Philip Blond, *Red Tory – how the left and right have broken Britain and how we can fix it,* Faber & Faber, London, 2010.

57 Rowena Davis, *Tangled up in Blue – Blue Labour and the struggle for Labour's soul,* Ruskin, London, 2011.

58 John Milbank, *Theology and Social Theory: Beyond Secular Reason,* 2nd edition: Blackwell, Oxford, 2006; Milbank, Pickstock and Ward (eds), *Radical Orthodoxy: A new theology,* Routledge, Abingdon, 1999. For an brief, accessible introduction to Milbank's thought, see an online interview entitled 'Theologians in conversation: the big society' http://www.youtube.com/watch?v=fE2cPQ5lqy8

rather than the right, though it dismisses these categories as part of the problem it wants to solve. But like the Religious Right it denounces 'secularism' and sociology. These are the means for humankind to escape its covenant with God through a system of thought that explains itself without reference to God, it suggests. Radical Orthodoxy is one of the set of religious projects that seek to penetrate the political system to restore a covenant with God – a covenant that secular thought has been destroying since the eighteenth century Enlightenment.

State of AnGeLs

In New York City, it is 13th September 2001.

The day before yesterday, Al Qaeda hurled two fully laden airliners into the city's World Trade Centre, bringing down the twin towers and killing nearly 3000 people. In a television studio, the breakfast show's guest is Anne Graham Lotz, second daughter of the celebrated evangelist Billy Graham. Anne markets items such as the *Expecting to see Jesus Bible study package* (ten participant guides, a DVD and a signed book, priced at $109.00) under the brand name AnGeL Ministries (motto: 'Giving you Jesus'). The interviewer, Jane Clayson, asks why a benevolent God allowed the attack to happen. The AnGeL leader explains

> for several years now Americans in a sense have shaken their fist at God and said, God, we want you out of our schools, our government, our business, we want you out of our marketplace. And God, who is a gentleman, has just quietly backed out of our national and political life, our public life. Removing his hand of blessing and protection. We need to turn to God first of all and say, God, we're sorry we have treated you this way and we invite you now to come into our national life. We put our trust in you. We have our trust in God on our coins, we need to practice it.

Four years later, after the waters unleashed by Hurricane Katrina overwhelmed the flood defences of New Orleans, Anne's words were repeated on many Christian websites, as words of prophecy whose warnings were again being fulfilled.

George W Bush was elected President in 2000. Soon his team downgraded internal counter-insurgency work in the chain of command reporting to him on security matters. When intelligence arrived about Saudi students in a private flying school learning to pilot (but not land) large aircraft, expert warnings of a coming attack were lost among the competing voices jostling for attention in the President's new system.

He was re-elected in 2004. In 2005, Katrina proved disastrous because the US Army engineers responsible for flood protection works in New Orleans had made serious errors while saving $100m by cutting the standards of the defences in works carried out in the 1990s. Thousands of lives were lost and two long and costly wars followed from the first muddle. Thousands of lives were lost once more as a result of the second mistake.[59]

President Bush won each election after campaigning successfully for the support of Christians. In both, he led by 2:1 among regular churchgoers, and his main opponent held the equivalent lead among non-churchgoers.[60] Disasters followed each election, in 2001 and 2005. But the President, his predecessors and their teams are, according to the AnGeL whose business is *Giving you Jesus*, not responsible; the incompetence of government is, apparently, the will of a god rejected by a faithless citizenry.

Whether the disasters were a judgment by God on those voting against President Bush, or those who had decided to elect him, or both, seems an odd and unhelpful speculation. The fact is that while the state could not prevent terrorists planning to seize civil aircraft, or a particularly nasty hurricane arriving on the east coast, neither event needed to come as a surprise. The catastrophic consequences were well within the ability of a competent state to prevent. The disasters were a result of negligence in public office – fairly basic and avoidable failures not necessarily on the part of President Bush personally, but certainly by the state machine.

The political anthropologist Georges Balandier reports that the basis of all states is that "sovereigns are the kinsmen of the gods".[61] Rick Santorum's call for a "Jesus candidate" to stand against the "economy candidate" reminds us of an idea as ancient as politics itself, an idea reiterated by the voice of AnGeL in that TV studio – that the management of public affairs is not properly placed with people just because they are capable of doing the work. Political leaders have to deal with the powerful forces that decide whether humans prosper or perish, whose 'hand of protection' may be withdrawn if the gods become displeased. So when Christians hear that their leaders must be, in Balandier's phrase, "kinsmen of the gods", they should not take this as a finding with biblical roots. It should not be assumed to be founded on Christian principles. Rather it comes from a *political* belief that all

59   For the role of human negligence in America's catastrophes of 2001 and 2005, see Laurence Wright, *The Looming Tower: al Queda's road to 9/11*, Penguin books, Harmondsworth, 2007; and Rogers, Kemp, Bosworth and Seed, 'Interaction between the US Army Corps of Engineers and the Orleans Levy Board preceding the drainage canal wall failures and catastrophic flooding of New Orleans in 2005', in *Water Policy*, vol. 17, no. 4 (2015): http://levees.org/2/wp-content/uploads/2015/11/WPOL-V17-NO4-21051.pdf
60   http://www.people-press.org/2004/12/06/religion-and-the-presidential-vote/
61   Georges Balandier, translated A M Sheridan Smith, *Political Anthropology*, Penguin, Harmondsworth, 1972, p99.

authority must be validated by religion. For followers of this instinct, rulers in a state are always a kind of priesthood, mediators with God or the gods or "some god". The job of the state, on this account, is to bring about the conditions that will satisfy this god, rather than exercise skills in government and administration. Its leaders are "kinsmen of the gods".

In spite of having contributed so much to our civilization and providing its foundation, the Christian Faith is in danger of being stealthily and subtly brushed aside. The evidence has been mounting in recent years. Teachers and council employees are suspended for offering to 'say a prayer'. A devoted nurse is banned from wearing a cross, a British Airways worker told to remove hers. Roman Catholic adoption agencies are closed down under new laws. Christian marriage registrars who cannot, in good conscience, preside over civil partnership ceremonies are summarily dismissed.

So, it appears that flowing from a combination of well-meaning political correctness, multiculturalism and overt opposition to Christianity, a new climate, hostile to our country's tradition and history, is developing.

Yet in the last census, 72% identified themselves as Christians.

Lord Carey, former Archbishop of Canterbury,
writing in support of the Not Ashamed campaign: 2011

Chapter 2

Court in the act

In bed with the Bulls

On Thursday 4th September 2008, Steven Preddy was planning a seaside weekend for himself, his partner and their new dog, a miniature Schnauzer – a companion not accepted into many hotels. Phoning from his Bristol home, he found, he thought, just the right place – the Chymorvah Hotel on the sensationally beautiful coast at Marazion in Cornwall. The partners and their dog duly arrived the next night. To their surprise, they were turned away. Steven's partner was Martyn Hall. The Chymorvah Hotel policy was that guests cannot share a double bed unless their relationship conforms to the Christian model of marriage ("being the union of one man to one woman for life to the exclusion of all others"), affirmed by Mr and Mrs Bull,[62] the owners of the hotel, and stated on their website, in the section used to make online bookings.

The policy would have allowed these guests (and their dog) to share one of their other rooms. The Chymorvah had seven rooms, including two 'twins' furnished with single beds. These 'twin' rooms – for sharing by people who are not married – were already booked. The staff person apologised for the misunderstanding – he had not explained the policy on the phone and the visitors had not used the website – and refunded Steven's deposit. Steven, Martyn and the dog departed, and found another place to stay.

Steven and Martyn took the Bulls to court under the Equality Act (Sexual Orientation) Regulations 2007, which made it illegal for anyone providing a service to discriminate on grounds of sexuality.[63] They were supported by the Equality and Human Rights Commission. The Bulls' defence was funded by the Legal Defence Fund of the Christian Institute, the charity existing to "promote Christian influence in a secular world".

In January 2011, a judge in Bristol found in favour of Steven and Martyn's claim. The fact that the hotel's policy applied to heterosexual (but unmarried) couples as well as to same-sex partners was not ac-

---

62 Sadly Mr Peter Bull died in 2016: http://www.christian.org.uk/news/peter-bull-1939-2016-he-finished-his-race/
63 These regulations were later replaced by the 2010 Equality Act, which brought together a range of anti-discrimination law built up since racial discrimination was first outlawed in the 1960s.

cepted as a defence. The county court judge found that Mr and Mrs Bull were guilty of direct discrimination on grounds of sexual orientation. He ordered Mr and Mrs Bull to pay both Steven and Martyn £1,800 each in compensation for their injured feelings. However he did accept that his ruling raised issues of law. The Bulls argued that, even if they had discriminated against their would-be guests, they were protected by the European Convention on Human Rights which grants the right to freedom of religion and the right to a private life. They said that allowing unmarried people to share a double bed, and thus to have sex in their hotel, would be a violation of their religious freedom and that the effect would be that they would lose their livelihood as a result of their religious belief. They also argued that the hotel was their own home and therefore that their privacy would be invaded if they were required to accept unmarried couples into their double beds.

The Bulls' appeal against the Bristol court's finding was considered at the Royal Courts of Justice on 8th and 9th November 2011. For the appeal, as for the County Court hearing, the Christian Institute appointed James Dingemans QC, a highly distinguished barrister who earlier in his career was hailed as a "star" by the *Daily Telegraph* while serving as counsel to the high-profile Hutton Inquiry.[64] The Court of Appeal considered that the Bulls did indeed discriminate, unlawfully, against Steven and Martyn. The couple could not meet the Bulls' standard of marriage, and therefore qualify for a double bed in the Chymorvah, for one reason – that they were of the same gender. Therefore, the discrimination was on grounds of sexuality only and unlawful under the 2007 regulations.

The court heard and recorded the Bulls' conviction, based on their Christian faith, that all sexual relations outside marriage were sinful. Offering double beds to unmarried couples meant supporting this sin, and if so obliged, they would have to close and lose their business. The court did not accept that the Bulls' right to a private life entitled them to refuse a double bed to Steven and Martyn: the rooms were advertised for booking and were therefore offered as open to the public. Nor did they accept the argument based on freedom of religion – the right to free expression of religion is restricted by "such limitations as are prescribed by law and are necessary in a democratic society in the interests of public safety, for the protection of public order, health or morals, or for the protection of the rights and freedoms of others"[65] so

---

64 *Daily Telegraph* 7th September 2003. The Hutton Inquiry was an investigation into the death of Dr David Kelly, a government scientist who bled to death after being named as the source for information used in a BBC reporter's claim that the Prime Minister Tony Blair had exaggerated evidence to justify the invasion of Iraq.
65 Article 9(2) of the European Convention on Human Rights.

they could not refuse the double bed on religious grounds if this meant denying their guests a right established in the regulations. The appeal was dismissed.

The Christian Institute appointed James Dingemans QC and his team in another case with similarities to that of Chymorvah, as well as one or two differences. In March 2010, Michael Black booked the 'Zurich' room with a double bed, one of three rooms advertised at the Swiss Bed and Breakfast in Cookham, Berkshire. The proprietor is Mrs Susanne Wilkinson whose husband Mike is pastor of the MCF Community church in Marlowe. As Mrs Wilkinson explained to the *Daily Mail*:[66] "I'd had a booking from a Mr Black for the Zurich room — a nice big double with an en-suite, and, naturally, I assumed it was for Mr and Mrs Black. But as I helped them manoeuvre their car into the drive, I realised they were two men." Mrs Wilkinson invited them in, explained they would not be accepted to share a bed because of her religious convictions and returned their deposit. "I am not a hotel, I am a guest house and this is a private house" she told the CI. With the support of the civil rights organisation Liberty, Michael Black and his partner John Morgan took the Wilkinsons to court. In September 2012, Reading County Court found unlawful discrimination on grounds of sexual orientation, and awarded each claimant £1800 – the same as in the Chymorvah case.

There are some differences between the two cases. For one thing, the Swiss Bed and Breakfast is a smaller establishment where the proprietors' private areas are closer to the rooms offered to paying guests. For another, Steve and Martyn, the Chymorvah claimants, were in a civil partnership;[67] Michael and John, the Swiss Bed and Breakfast claimants, were a long term couple, but, at the time of their failed attempt to share the Zurich room, were not in a civil partnership. Could this be significant? One judge hearing the Chymorvah appeal did find that the Bulls "are not obliged to provide double bedded rooms at all, but if they do, then they must be prepared to let them to homosexual couples, *at least if they are in a civil partnership*,[68] as well as to heterosexual married couples". This left scope for a hotel to refuse couples if they are neither married nor in a civil partnership. But Mrs Wilkinson did not ask if Michael and John were civil partners, and this does not seem to have entered into the situation. She told the judge at Reading County Court, Recorder Claire Moulder, that while she had a prefer-

---

66 Posted on *Mail Online*, 21st September 2012.
67 Civil partnership, allowed since 2005, gave legal rights to same-sex partners similar to those enjoyed by married partners. Same-sex marriage was allowed in 2014, including a provision for a civil partnership to be converted to a marriage.
68 Author's italics.

ence for heterosexual couples to be married, "it is impossible to know whether a heterosexual couple is married ... and it would be offensive to pry into their personal lives either when booking or on arrival".

The first judge in the Chymorvah case – Judge Rutherford of Bristol County Court – described it as "a very clear example of how social attitudes have changed over the years for it is not so very long ago that these beliefs of the defendants would have been those accepted as normal by society at large". In a booklet describing how Christians are 'marginalised', the Christian Institute said: "A Christian couple who run a guesthouse in Cornwall are being sued under equality laws because they have a well-advertised policy of allowing only married couples to book double rooms." This is slightly but significantly misleading. The Chymorvah policy does in fact allow an unmarried couple to share a double room – provided the furniture includes two separate single beds. The 'changing attitudes' mentioned by Judge Rutherford have a curious twist. Yes, a few decades ago, with recent memories of gay sex as a crime, a policy of excluding active homosexuals from hotel bedrooms might not have caused a stir. But anyone switching on their TV at Christmas would see the most popular comedy partnership of the day, Morecambe and Wise, sharing a double bed in a regular sketch. It signified an intimate and trusting relationship; the audience was not expected to imagine the two entertainers having sex together. And on another night another comedy, usually one made in the USA, might show a heterosexual married couple in separate single beds: no one assumed that this signified a lowering of their sexual appetites. Part of 'changing attitudes' seems to be an assumption that any two people sharing a double bed are necessarily there to have sex, and even more strangely, that the space between two separate beds in the same room forms a reliable barrier against sexual union.

Council at prayer: Bone of contention

While the appeal judges were digesting the legal implications of the Chymorvah Hotel double-bed policy, Bideford Town Council, a local parish council in Devon, held its usual monthly meeting, on the second Thursday of November. At 6.30pm, the Mayor opened the evening's business by inviting Father Terry O'Donovan of the Sacred Heart church to lead the first Agenda item, entitled 'Prayers.' The town council had included 'Prayers' on its Agenda since 1988 (and intermittently before, since 1941).

In 2007 Clive Bone joined the council as a Liberal Democrat repre-senting South ward. In 2008 he twice failed to get 'Prayers' removed from the council agenda. The National Secular Society, as part of its campaign against prayer in council meetings, joined Mr Bone – who by this time had left the council – in taking its objection to the Royal Courts of Justice, where in the Administrative Court Mr Justice Ouseley considered the case on 2nd December 2011. As he had for the ear-lier Chymorvah double-bed appeal, the distinguished 'silk' James Dingemans QC appeared for Bideford Town Council, with the Christian Institute footing the bill.

The court heard that Prayers, led by various religious leaders, took place, before any other business, and that members could leave for this item without being recorded as absent from the meeting. So far, this looks like a short gathering *prior* to a meeting – an arrangement for 'prayers' that is common in parish councils; the 'prayers' do not form part of the agenda – the meeting does not start until afterwards and the prayers are not recorded in the minutes. It makes no difference whether councillors are present or not, as technically the event is not part of the agenda. The National Secular Society told the court that they do not object to that arrangement. But in Bideford's case, 'Prayers' was listed as an Agenda item and recorded in the minutes. Members were summoned by the clerk to attend Prayers – but they could walk out without being recorded as absent. This was, the judge said, contradic-tory. Either the praying was part of the Agenda and therefore legally considered as something the council did in order to "transact its busi-ness" or they were something else.

The court dismissed the National Secular Society's claim that Prayers on the agenda amounted either to discrimination or a breach of Mr Bone's human rights. Under section 111 of the Local Government Act, the council's meeting includes anything necessary to get the coun-cil's job done, and it was clear that the council did not in practice treat them as necessary for that purpose – as otherwise it could not have al-lowed members to absent themselves without explanation. However, the court also found that the council did not have power to put prayer on the agenda since it could not reasonably be held in a secular society that praying together was necessary to enable the council to "transact its business". A council is not empowered to hold prayers as part of its agenda, and this part of the National Secular Society's case was ac-cepted.

The judgments in these two cases:

THE QUEEN ON THE APPLICATION OF NATIONAL SECULAR SOCIETY
(1st claimant) and MR CLIVE BONE (2nd Claimant) -v- BIDEFORD TOWN
COUNCIL

and

BULL & BULL -v- HALL AND PREDDY -

were both published on 10th February 2012.

The next day, 11th February 2012, a number of leading British national newspapers linked them in their main, front page printed stories. **Christianity under attack: anger as court rulings go against British worshippers** boomed the headline on the *Daily Mail*. The headline in *The Times* newspaper read **Christianity on the rack as judge bans public prayer**. Its story quoted Lord Carey, the former Archbishop of Canterbury as being "horrified. The Christian voice is being silenced ... the marginalisation of Christianity is hollowing out our value system and our culture".

The Christian Institute published a press release quoting politicians and church leaders on the subject of the Bideford ruling:

MPs have criticised an "utterly preposterous" High Court ruling that says it is illegal to say prayers as a 'formal' part of local council meetings.

Eric Pickles, the Communities Secretary, disputed the basis of the ruling and said that the "right to worship is a fundamental and hard fought British liberty".

Chris Bryant, the Labour MP for Rhondda, branded the ruling as "utterly preposterous", and said that he would "consider" tabling a bill to oppose the ruling himself.

Conservative MP Tim Loughton said: "If you don't like prayers at council meetings don't go to them – simple. But don't spoil it for the majority who do appreciate it".

Fellow Tory David Jones said that he would "not be surprised" if the ruling led to a challenge to the practice of saying prayers in Parliament.

And the Bishop of Exeter, the Right Reverend Michael Langrish, said: "I think it's a great pity that a tiny minority are seeking to ban the majority, many of whom find prayers very, very helpful, from continuing with a process in which no-one actually has to participate."

Earlier this morning the High Court ruled that the saying of prayers as a 'formal' part of local council meetings was unlawful.

The judge said: "The saying of prayers as part of the formal meeting of a Council is not lawful under s111 of the Local Government Act 1972, and there is no statutory power permitting the practice to continue."

But Mr Pickles disputed this assertion on his Twitter feed saying that the

"Localism Act gives councils power of general competence, logically this includes ability to pray before meetings".

The practice of saying prayers at Bideford Town Council meetings is understood to date back to the days of Queen Elizabeth the First. The Council has, recently, twice voted in support of continuing with the prayers.

Individual councillors were free to not take part in the prayers if they wished, and the register of attendance was not taken until after the prayers had finished.

Bideford Town Council legal defence was underwritten by the Christian Institute – a national charity that defends religious liberty.

Simon Calvert, a spokesman for The Christian Institute, said: "There is no way that Parliament, when it passed the Local Government Act 40 years ago, intended it to be used to outlaw prayers.

"This case was brought by a campaign group that wants to drive Christianity out of public life, and the High Court has today given them great encouragement to take matters further.

"It is high time Parliament put a stop to this assault upon our national heritage. What's next? Will prayers at the cenotaph end up in court?

"What about local councils that wish to formally mark the Queen's Diamond Jubilee as part of their official meeting? Is that now unlawful too?"

Within a week the Government responded to this furore with the following announcement:

Eric Pickles gives councils back the freedom to pray

Local Government Secretary Eric Pickles today (18 February 2012) gave local councils a major new power that will allow town halls to continue to hold prayers.

Local councils now have a power that should enable them to continue to include prayers as part of the formal business at council meetings, if they wish, and thereby maintain the common practice in council meetings across the country.

This responds to last week's High Court ruling against Bideford Town Council based on an interpretation of Section 111 of the Local Government Act 1972 rather than on equality or human rights grounds. It judged that councils did not have the powers to hold prayers as part of formal business.

This major new legal power is contained in the Coalition Government's Localism Act 2011, which creates a 'general power of competence' that will allow councils to legally do anything an individual could do unless specifically prohibited by law. This should give councils that want to continue holding formal prayers the confidence and legal standing to do so.

Mr Pickles has fast-tracked and personally signed a Parliamentary Commencement Order so the new power can be exercised by all major local authorities in England from today and following due Parliamentary process for parishes by April.

Today's intervention builds on the speech by the Prime Minister in Christ

Church, Oxford, in December, where he asserted: "We are a Christian country and we should not be afraid to say so". It also follows the official Ministerial delegation to the Holy See this week led by Cabinet Minister, Baroness Warsi; in her speech, she criticised the intolerance of "militant secularisation".

Eric Pickles, Secretary of State for Communities and Local Government, said:

"The High Court judgement has far wider significance than just the municipal agenda of Bideford Town Council. For too long, faith has been marginalised in public life, undermining the very foundations of the British nation.

"As a matter of urgency I have personally signed a Parliamentary order to bring into force an important part of the new Localism Act – the general power of competence – that gives councils the vital legal standing that should allow them to continue to hold formal prayers at meetings where they wish to do so.

"This should effectively overtake the ruling and it also shows that greater localism can give local councils the strength and freedom to act in their best interests.

"We will stand for freedom to worship, for Parliamentary sovereignty, and for long-standing British liberties."

So it was claimed that the High Court was driving Christianity out of public life, by banning a tradition of holding prayers; that there was a threat of this ban extending to Parliament, where both Commons and Lords open their daily business with Christian prayer; that politicians of all persuasions were determined to reinstate prayers; and that Secretary Pickles sprang to the rescue with 'urgency' by signing an order overtaking the ruling of the Court. But was any of this true? Was there in fact any contention about the High Court's ruling? The CI in its press release said that councillors were "free not to take part" in prayer, and that the register of attendance was not taken until after the praying was done. As Tim Loughton MP noted, the 'simple' truth was that if a councillor did not like prayer, he or she did not need to come along. This was exactly what the Court observed – which meant that it was not, in fact, part of the agenda. It was claimed that the ruling threatened praying in Parliament. Ex-Archbishop Lord Carey and his son wrote that there was no difference between prayer appearing on the Parliamentary order papers and on the agenda of a town or parish council. But in fact there is a big difference. The Houses of Parliament are legislative bodies (they mainly exist to pass laws) meeting throughout the day for much of the year, with hundreds of members most of whom are not present most of the time, but rush in when summoned by bells to votes. Bideford council is not a house of Parliament. It is one of many thousand 'town and parish councils' which form the lowest level in the hierarchy of elected councils. Parish councils may also be called community, neighbourhood, or village councils. They are not 'local authorities' – this term is reserved for the more powerful district, county, unitary and borough councils that provide essential local services. Town and parish councils exist widely in the more rural parts of the United Kingdom; in many cities they do not exist at all. A typical town or parish council has a dozen or so members who meet once or twice a month for an hour or two. It does not pass laws: it makes decisions concerning graveyards, parks, footpaths, youth clubs, carparks, public toilets, play areas and such local matters. To pay for its work, it raises money through a 'precept' on the local property taxes, as police and fire authorities also do. In parish councils, unlike the Houses of Parliament, members do not wander in and out or just pop in to vote and then disappear: this would be totally unacceptable. If they miss meetings they have to submit apologies with reasons that the council accepts.

In the Bideford case, the Court found, the council did not require members to be present for praying, so it obviously did not in fact treat praying as part of its agenda, so it was not, from a legal standpoint, part of the agenda. Councillor Bone had no case for discrimination, since he was not missing anything – he did not need to show up, it made no difference whether he showed up or not, and nothing was decided that was part of the business of the council. The Christian Institute, the National Secular Society and Tim Loughton MP all in fact agree that councils can if they wish have Christian prayers – as Mr Pickles also said in his Twitter feed – '*before*' the meeting. The Christian Institute could have said, and would have been more accurate had it said, that the National Secular Society and Councillor Bone had lost their claim of discrimination and indeed had wasted the time of the High Court by implying that he was required to attend an activity that was in truth entirely voluntary.

But what about Eric Pickles' claim to have changed the law so as to "effectively overtake" the Court's ruling? Thus rescuing faith from marginalisation and the "very foundations of the nation" from being undermined? What was that about? The following is rather technical but necessary to make sense of what was going on.

Until the Local Government Act 2000, councils could only do things that were specifically required or permitted by law: if they decided to try to do something else, they had to go to Parliament and ask for a new law to be passed to allow it. The 2000 Act gave Local Authorities the 'power of wellbeing' which meant the ability to do anything for the general economic, social or environmental good of their area. Town and Parish councils did not have access to this power until 2007, when, in the Local Government and Public Involvement in Health Act, section 77 extended the 'power of wellbeing' to 'eligible' town and parish councils. 'Eligible' here was left to the Secretary of State, with Parliamentary approval, to define. The resulting order was that eligibility meant achieving 'quality parish council' status – the main conditions of this being that a set proportion of all its councillors have stood for election (rather than being co-opted by the elected members, as many parish councillors are) and that the council's paid administrator (the Clerk) had a recognised qualification. In 2011 the Localism Act gave all Local Authorities the 'general power of competence', which effectively means doing anything they wish (without the previous limitation that it had to be for public 'wellbeing'). This included 'eligible' parish councils as defined by the Secretary of State. Mr Pickles' order, signed in time to be approved by Parliament and come into law on 27th March 2012, reproduced very much the same rules for 'eligibility' as existed under the previous 'quality parish council' scheme. Bideford Town Council was a quality council under the 2007 Act criteria; so it already had the power to do anything for the wellbeing of its community. *If* the 2011 Act gave new power to Bideford Town Council – power that it did not have under the 2007 Act – then the implication is that praying was not the for the 'wellbeing' of Bideford but served some narrower purpose. But in fact this was irrelevant to the case. The Court's finding that Bideford Town Council lacked the power to pray could not have been 'overtaken' by any legislation extending the powers of councils. The point of the ruling was that, in holding prayers when attendance was voluntary and not even recorded, the council as such was not *doing* anything at all.

Meanwhile the Christian Institute announced its intention to appeal the Bideford ruling. At its meeting on 8th February, Bideford Town Council held prayers as usual. The minutes show that under this item, this took the form of a moment of reflection supervised by the Religious Society of Friends (Quakers). The meeting also considered, and agreed, a request from the BBC to come to the next meeting and film the prayers. However if it came to make this film, the BBC would be disappointed, for no prayers are recorded on the agenda of this or any subsequent session of Bideford Town Council. On 8th March 2012, the council considered many matters including the progress of a children's centre, nuisance from a building site and funding to improve local shopping. Then it went into confidential session. One councillor withdrew. The minutes record:

> Members considered, at length, the terms of the offer from the Christian Institute to provide costs indemnity for the judicial review appeal.
>
> Proposed by Councillor Wootton, seconded and
>
> RESOLVED: That the Council does not accept the terms of the indemnity and that the lodged appeal be withdrawn.

This was carried by 8 votes to 5.

Councillor Bone makes one further appearance in the annals of Bideford Town Council: on 18th December 2014, the Mayor led a minute's silence to mark the passing of former councillor Clive Bone.

Earlier in 2014, Lady Warsi[69] resigned from the Government in protest over its foreign policy. Her place as Faith Minister was taken by Eric Pickles. *Evangelicals Now,* a monthly paper widely read in British churches of the evangelical persuasion, reported this in its September issue, noting with the authority of the Christian Institute that

> In February 2012, Pickles fast-tracked new laws to override a High Court's decision to ban councils from having prayers at official meetings. A local atheist ex-councillor had sued Bideford Town Council over prayers being said at meetings. Pickles' actions after the case led to a circular, which said that all major local authorities in England could continue to hold prayers at formal meetings.

But in fact this was not so. No new laws were 'fast-tracked' to 'override' the High Court decision; Bideford had no new powers; it stopped putting prayer on its agenda and dropped its legal action. The Christian Institute and its network gave credibility to a political gesture empty of any practical effect. Councils continue, where they wish, to hold prayers before meetings. In the Houses of Parliament, prayer continues on the order paper. The Parliament website explains how this happens:

> The Speaker's Chaplain usually reads the prayers. The form of the main prayer is as follows:
>
> "Lord, the God of righteousness and truth, grant to our Queen and her government, to Members of Parliament and all in positions of responsibility, the guidance of your Spirit. May they never lead the nation wrongly through love of power, desire to please, or unworthy ideals but laying aside all private interests and prejudices keep in mind their responsibility to seek to improve the condition of all mankind; so may your kingdom come and your name be hallowed. Amen" ...
>
> MPs and Peers stand for prayers facing the wall behind them. It is thought this practice developed due to the difficulty Members would historically have faced

---

69 A Conservative and a Muslim, she served as a minister within the Department of Communities and Local Government in the Coalition government.

of kneeling to pray while wearing a sword.

On a personal note, I spent ten years as a member of a parish council in Shropshire. When I first joined, the chair was occupied by a man who spoke Russian and ran the local Labour Party, and had a somewhat exaggerated reputation among the local Freemasons as a supposed communist. After he retired from the council, an influential Conservative (and Freemason) councillor said we had become too informal, so we should reinstate an earlier practice of holding prayers before the start of meetings. In a secret ballot on the proposal to restore prayer, I voted against. While I had nothing against more formality, as a Christian I did not favour the use of prayer as a public ritual in a secular setting. But the motion was passed and then at the start of meetings a prayer, typed on a card, would be read out by the chair or another councillor. Later I took over the chair and often led the prayers. This I did in my usual way, following what the local Anglican Bishop called the 'evangelical' style – speaking conversationally to my God in the name of his risen Son. I did not read from a card but no one seemed to mind. Everyone stood up to hear the prayers. Perhaps parish councillors, like Members of Parliament, have to take care not to interfere with their imaginary swords.

The conscience of Lillian Ladele

In December 2005, the Civil Partnerships Act came into force. It allowed couples of the same gender to register their relationship and achieve most of the legal protections offered by marriage. The Christian Institute saw the Act as creating a "form of counterfeit marriage" and, in common with many voices across Christian opinion, campaigned against it. Once it was implemented, local authorities had, by law, to publish lists of 'civil partnership registrars' to deal with the formal business of recording and registering new partnerships. Lillian Ladele worked in Islington council, in north London, where she had been a registrar for three years. When she came back from sick leave in November 2005, she found herself on the civil partnership registrars list, along with all the other registrars in the borough. Lillian was among three registrars with an objection to this. As a Christian, Lillian later wrote, she felt that registering a civil partnership would be to "facilitate the formation of a union ... contrary to God's law". Of the other two, one, Fatima was a Muslim sessional worker who left the service. The other, Theresa, a Christian, accepted a new role, with protected pay, as a receptionist.

At first Lillian was able to swap shifts with colleagues to avoid the unwelcome work. In March 2006, two registrars (both themselves gay) complained that they were being victimised by Lillian's avoidance tactics. Council managers warned Lillian that she was in breach of the council's 'dignity for all' policy and could face dismissal for gross misconduct for discriminating against customers on the basis of their sexuality. Lillian maintained that her religious objections should be accommodated. If not, it was she who was facing discrimination on the grounds of religion. The issue rumbled on, down the familiar boggy path through staff meetings and team-building at awaydays. Managers' plans to discipline Lillian were discussed at Islington Lesbian Gay Bisexual Transgender Forum, in breach of confidentiality. She complained about this and other action which she found discriminatory, but the council did not investigate her complaints. She was told that her own statement of her religious views – and her request to be excused civil partnership duties – constituted 'gross misconduct', and that if she continued to take this line, she would be dismissed. With the support of the CI, and represented by its 'star' barrister James Dingemans QC, Lillian took her case to an Employment Tribunal. Evidence showed that some other councils made arrangements for Muslim and Christian registrars to keep their jobs without doing civil partnerships. In July 2008 the Tribunal found that she had suffered discrimination and harassment at the hands of Islington council due to her religious beliefs. Islington council appealed this decision, and the Employment Appeals Tribunal found in favour of Islington and overturned the previous decision. Lillian went to the Appeal Court which heard the case at the end of 2009. By this time Lillian had resigned as a registrar at Islington.

The core of Lillian's case, accepted by the first Tribunal, was that there was a conflict between two sets of rights: on the one hand of gay people not to experience unfavourable treatment due to sexual preference, on the other of religious people not to experience unfavourable treatment due to their faith. Which side holds the 'trump' in this standoff? To Lillian, the solution was for Islington to do as some other councils had, and arrange their staff rotas so that they could accommodate her religious views while still enabling gay couples to register their relationships. The first Tribunal found that failing to offer this solution meant Islington was treating her less favourably than other employees, and this discrimination was due to Lillian's religious belief. The

Appeal Tribunal threw this argument out, for reasons that the higher Appeal court memorably supported in paragraph 29 of its judgment (here the ET is the Employment Tribunal, the EAT is the Employment Appeals Tribunal and Elias J is the senior Judge at the EAT):

> The ET's conclusion that Ms Ladele suffered direct discrimination on the core issue, namely, by being required by Islington to conduct civil partnerships, is as the EAT said, in paragraph 52 of Elias J's impressive and cogent judgment, "quite unsustainable". As he went on to explain, Ms Ladele's complaint "is not that she was treated differently from others; rather it was that she was not treated differently when she ought to have been", and her complaint was "about a failure to accommodate her difference, rather than a complaint that she is being discriminated against because of that difference". As Elias J said in the next paragraph of his judgment, "[i]t cannot constitute direct discrimination to treat all employees in precisely the same way". This error also applied to virtually all of the other findings of direct discrimination by the ET...

James Dingemans QC did not question this reasoning. He focused on more narrow issues, albeit ones that were important to Lillian's state of mind in all this – the breach of confidentiality (when managers leaked their intention to discipline her) and the claim that simply writing a polite letter explaining her views amounted to 'gross misconduct.' The court found that, while deplorable, these actions were not a result of discrimination on grounds of religion. Looking at the issue more generally, the court stated that it was not Lillian's religious *belief* that caused managers to take action against her: it was her *action* – her refusal to do the work requested of her.

Lillian took her case to Europe. On 3rd September 2010, she put before the European Court of Human Rights her complaint that the law of the United Kingdom had failed to protect her against discrimination, violating her rights under the European Convention on Human Rights. Her plea was considered in conjunction with three others tabled from June to September 2010, in a case known as Eweida and Others v the United Kingdom. Still supported by the CI, Lillian was now represented by Dinah Rose QC, a prominent, liberal lawyer regarded by Human Rights campaigners as the "the finest advocate of her generation".[70] Lillian's argument was that by refusing to excuse her from conducting civil partnership duty, Islington was breaching her rights under Article 14 of the Convention, which says:

> The enjoyment of the rights and freedoms set forth in this Convention shall be secured without discrimination...

---

70 Tiger at the Bar: QC who helped win the fight to see Charles's letters, *Guardian* 27 March 2015.

Lillian's case then referred to Article 9:

> Everyone has the right to freedom of thought, conscience and religion...

The court agreed that making Lillian take civil partnership work, something she had not agreed to and was not an original condition of her employment, had a "particular detriment" for her. However it did not find that Islington had been disproportionate or unreasonable in requiring all its registrars to take this work, given that it was also trying to meet the needs of all its customers who had a right to be treated equally. But two judges (of seven on the bench) registered disagreement. Judge Nebojša Vucinic (from Montenegro) and Vincent A. De Gaetano (from Malta) placed on record an interesting opinion based on the word *conscience* found in Article 9. The case was 'not so much one of religious freedom', they said, but of Lillian's conscience:

> In essence it is a judgment of reason whereby a physical person recognises the moral quality of a concrete act ... We are of the view that once ... a *genuine* and *serious* case of conscientious objection is established, the State is obliged to respect the individual's freedom of conscience

Lillian had not imposed her views on anyone. No user of Islington's service had any reason even to notice, let alone complain about, her non-appearance at civil partnership formalities. Instead "back stabbing by her colleagues and blinkered political correctness" had meant she paid a high price for following her conscience, like the victims (according to a comparison made by the two judges) of Nazi firing squads and the Spanish Inquisition.

Reporting on the court proceedings and surrounding commentary, the Christian Institute said:

> Yesterday, the European Court of Human Rights ruled against Lillian Ladele, a registrar who was forced out of her job for refusing to conduct civil partnerships.

> The *Daily Mail* said it has "deep reservations" about the rulings, and says they "prove that the court's respect for our national religion and the right of believers to follow their consciences is paper-thin".

> Five judges rejected Lillian Ladele's claim, but two believed that she had suffered discrimination because of her Christian beliefs about marriage.

> The judges that dissented said her refusal to conduct civil partnerships was a "manifestation of her deep religious conviction and beliefs" and the state is obliged to make accommodation for her faith.

In fact, judges de Caetano and Vudinic carefully said something rather different from this version. They said:

> Although freedom of religion and freedom of conscience are dealt with under the same Article of the Convention, there is a fundamental difference between the two.

While in Lillian's case her conscience was guided by her faith, it was specifically the conscience that these judges wanted to protect – whether or not it had a religious motivation.

Does this distinction matter? It is significant, for this reason. If freedom of religion – in this case, specifically, the Christian faith – is at stake here, then Christians who act differently from Lillian are willing for Christian freedom to be sacrificed for the sake of preserving jobs or some other material gains. Lillian stands for her faith and is 'not ashamed'. The personal act of registering a civil partnership becomes, on this view, an act of disloyalty to the faith like denying the lordship of Christ or agreeing not to study the Bible – activities that are normally expected of Christians but that religiously oppressive regimes may try to restrict.

How might 'freedom of conscience' be different? The Apostle Paul wrote about conscience in a letter to the church in Corinth. His advice was requested on whether Christians should go into pagan temples and eat food that had been dedicated to idols. Some Christians found this against their conscience. That was plainly wrong – idols are powerless so it is safe to eat their food. Those who objected had, Paul said, 'weak' consciences. But that didn't necessarily mean other Christians, so confident of their faith as to have no problem sauntering into a pagan temple and munching the leftovers, should flaunt their liberty. They needed to be mindful of the upset they might cause, and not risk acting in a way that might damage the more fragile faith of their conscience-stricken fellow-believers.

Lillian said: 'I feel unable to directly facilitate the formation of a union that I sincerely feel is contrary to God's law.' Judges de Caetano and Vudinic found this 'matter of conscience' so strongly felt that she should have been spared these duties. This prompted a debate in legal circles. Lady Hale, a judge of the UK Supreme Court, spoke about this in a thoughtful lecture on Human Rights in June 2014.[71] How far, she was asking herself, should the law go:

> in making special provisions or exceptions for particular beliefs, how far it should require the providers of employments, goods and services to accom-

---

71 https://www.supremecourt.uk/docs/speech-140613.pdf

modate them, and how far it should allow for a 'conscience clause', either to the providers, as argued by the hotel keepers in Bull v Hall, or to employees, as suggested by the dissenting minority in Ladele. I am not sure that our law has yet found a reasonable accommodation of all these different strands. The story has just begun.

If the law is to protect conscience, does that mean everyone's conscience, however motivated? Some argue, says Lady Hale, for particular protection for religious feelings. But does that mean *any* religion? It is obvious where this might lead – for instance to discrimination against Christians where they offend the consciences of others. One solution to this, as Lady Hale finds offered by former Bishop Michael Nazir-Ali, is to privilege Christianity in the legal system. She does not think this can be done. Is it either possible or right for Christians to argue that the law should protect Christian consciences but not others?

Lillian sincerely felt "unable to directly facilitate the formation of a union ... contrary to God's law". The Apostle Paul warns us not to use reason to the point where we disrespect the faith of others. But in Lady Hale's "story that has just begun", the conscience of Lillian Ladele may have far-reaching consequences for the rest of us, Christians and others. It may be kinder to Lillian to stay quiet. But it may also be taken to show that some are simply too 'ashamed' to support the quest for Christian legal privilege.

So – was Lillian's conscience telling her the truth? Here is the reason for answering 'no' – for thinking that Lillian is like those Corinthians whose weak consciences stopped them eating food dedicated to idols. Registrars do not act on their own account: they are agents of the state making official records. The unions they register do not start in front of the registration books: they have been, and continue to be, 'facilitated' not by the registrar, but by a pair of individuals, and the purpose of registration is simply to place on record, not the fact of the union, but the legal status and rights the state confers in particular conditions. Many registered unions may be 'contrary to God's law.' They may involve remarriage following a divorce – anyone who has spent time in any Christian community knows the wrestling with conscience that takes place over whether, and when, remarriage is 'contrary to God's law.' The reader can probably think of many things that might mean that a marriage is legal before the state but still a 'union contrary to God's law.' But we do not, as a society, expect paid registrars to make those judgments in the course of their work. Of course we might wish that Islington's management had taken a more relaxed view and let Lillian's conscience influence staff rotas, and it seems they would have done but for the complaints from other registrars – Dion Goncalves and Viktoria Kingsley – about the impact on them. But from a Christian standpoint, it is far from obvious that Lillian's conscience should have been accommodated as a matter of law, or that any of this needed to take up the time of the courts.

'On the way to theocracy': Eweida, Chaplin and Macfarlane

Three other cases were joined with Lillian's to make up the hearing of Eweida and Others v United Kingdom. All three applicants – Nadia Eweida, Shirley Chaplin and Gary Macfarlane – asked the European Court of Human Rights (ECHR) to find that UK law failed to uphold their Article 9 rights to religious freedom in connection with their employment. The two female claimants had employers who stopped them wearing a cross as visible jewellery, thus – in their view – denying them freedom to express their religion. The other, Gary, had been dismissed from his job as a therapist for failing, in his employer's view, to be prepared to treat gay customers equally. Nadia was supported by Liberty, a well-known secular organisation campaigning for civil liberty, and James Dingemans QC – who previously represented Lillian Ladele in the English courts – now led for Nadia's case. (Liberty had earlier intervened in support of Islington council in Lillian's case at the English Appeal court.) Gary and Shirley were supported by Christian Concern (CC) with a legal team led by Paul Diamond, and including the CC's Andrea Minichiello Williams and Andrew Marsh. Many bodies and individuals were permitted to make written interventions in the hearing, including the Alliance Defending Freedom (ADF) from the USA, former Archbishop Lord Carey and former Bishop Michael Nazir-Ali. Paul Coleman, ADF's legal counsel, joined Paul Diamond on the legal team for Gary and Shirley.

Nadia Eweida was a British Airways passenger services worker who was from the Egyptian Coptic Christian community. When the uniform had a high-necked blouse, she used to wear a cross on a chain round her neck under the uniform blouse. After a uniform change to an open necked blouse with a cravat in company colours, staff were required to keep jewellery under the cravat unless they had permission otherwise. For two years she complied. But she then started showing up at work with the cross visible, and eventually was sent home on unpaid leave. She turned down an offer of alternative, non-uniformed work and put in a grievance while a media storm broke over her plight. By the time BA amended its policy to permit religious and charitable symbols to be displayed, Nadia had been on unpaid leave for more than four months. She returned to work but took legal action against BA for discrimination. She failed in the English courts where judges put on record their concern at

> her insensitivity towards colleagues, her lack of empathy for those without a religious focus in their lives, and her incomprehension of the conflicting demands which professional management seeks to address and resolve on a near-daily basis.

She took her case to the ECHR. Hers was the only one of the four to succeed: the judges found there had been discrimination against her in breach of her Article 9 rights to express her religion, and that the "domestic authorities failed sufficiently to protect" her "right to manifest her religion". She was awarded costs and 2000 Euros for the hurt to her feelings. Her claim for compensation for lost wages, for the time when she chose to stay off work unpaid, was refused. In rejecting this, the court noted that "during the period … the applicant had enjoyed an income of well over twice the loss of earnings, some of it through gifts and donations, some as earnings from other sources". This did not deter the *Daily Mail*, in a lengthy and admiring celebration of her win, including this:[72]

> In 2006 BA suspended Nadia from her job without pay for five months after she refused to hide her cross. She tells me: "I still feel aggrieved. BA has never repaid me the salary I lost. It's very little to them — £3,900 — but it was my livelihood. I have a mortgage to pay. I'm waiting to see whether now they'll repay me."

Shirley Chaplin was a hospital nurse in Exeter. Her case resembled Nadia's. After a uniform change she was stopped from wearing jewellery that might cause hazard when working in close quarters with patients, and the effect was to stop her wearing a cross. She accepted a transfer to non-nursing duties in a job that was later cut. Courts heard that other Christians, and followers of other faiths, had complied with requests to remove insignia that did not comply with dress policy. Her applications to UK courts for relief on grounds of religious discrimination failed, and the ECHR rejected her appeal. Judges said that the hospital where she worked had health and safety grounds for its restriction, and stuck to this in the face of objections; this was different from the case of BA, which did not have such strong reasons for its position, as was proved when it changed it after protests.

---

72 BA had bullying lawyers, but I had God on my side: Inspiring interview with Heathrow worker who won the right to wear her cross at work – 19 January 2013.

Gary McFarlane was a counsellor with Relate in Bristol. He was a prominent member of a Christian church and made no secret of his conventionally Christian reservations on gay sexuality. For his first three years he gave relationship counselling which did not involve advice on sexual matters, and his clients included gay couples. He then took Relate's postgraduate diploma in psycho-sexual therapy (PST). After taking this course, he asked if he could not provide a PST service to gay couples. He was told this would not be possible within Relate's policies. At first he responded that he would be ready to provide these services. But after further discussions and challenges his manager concluded that what Gary had said about being ready to comply with the policy was not what he really meant or intended, and Gary was sacked. He claimed relief for wrongful dismissal and religious discrimination, but was not successful in the English courts on his claim that he had been unfavourably treated because of his religious views. The ECHR also found against him, seeing close parallels between his case and Lillian's. The two judges who gave the dissenting opinion, supporting Lillian, explained how they saw the difference between the two cases. Lillian, when she became a registrar, did not know or agree that she would have to register same-sex partnerships. Gary, all through his work with Relate, knew what was in the equalities policy.

Gary's case was particularly notable because of his line of defence and the intervention of Lord Carey, the former Archbishop of Canterbury. At his appeal to the Employment Appeals Tribunal, Gary was represented by two barristers: Paul Diamond, a leading adviser to CC and an international associate of ADF, and Thomas Cordrey, vice-chair of the Lawyers' Christian Fellowship (where Andrea Minichiello Williams was Director of Public Policy until setting up CC). As in the case of Lillian Ladele, the judges found that Gary lost his position at work not because of his Christian faith but because he was unwilling to do part of his job, and any employee, whatever their faith, would have suffered the same consequences: this could therefore not be put down to religious discrimination. In paragraph 17 of their judgement,[73] they went on to say:

> But the Claimant's case is that the Tribunal's approach involves an illegitimate distinction between the immediate conduct which led to the act complained of – that is, the Claimant's (perceived) unwillingness to counsel same-sex couples – and the religious belief of which that conduct was an outward and visible sign. As developed by Mr Cordrey, the underlying point is that for religious belief to be effectively protected it is necessary to prevent discrimination on

---

73 GG McFarlane (claimant) and Relate Avon Ltd (Respondent), EAT, judgement dated 30th November 2009.

the ground not only that a belief is held but that it is manifested. The importance of protecting not merely the right to hold religious beliefs but the right to manifest them in conduct was a recurrent theme of both his and Mr Diamond's submissions. The two are, they submitted, inseparable.

So the case presented by these Christian lawyers on Gary's behalf is that an action should be protected by law if it flows directly from a religious belief. The courts were not impressed by the legal strategy. Paul Diamond's

submissions were at a high level of generality and not closely related to any analysis of the particular issues on the appeal ... Although we found Mr Cordrey's submissions clear and helpful as far as they went, the procedure adopted was unsatisfactory ... it would have been helpful to have had a structured analysis of the key authorities, cross-referred to the particular issues arising on this appeal. That is not something which Mr Diamond offered us...

Gary's team then applied for permission to appeal to the higher Appeal Court. This was dismissed – the decision in Lillian Ladele's case established a precedent that must apply to Gary's. But "because of the wide issues raised", Lord Justice Laws gave time to responding to Paul Diamond's argument and to a submission that Lord Carey made to the court, "having regard to his seniority in the Church and the extent to which others may agree with his views".

Referring not just to Gary's case but also to the various others later taken to the ECHR, Lord Carey wrote:

I wish to dispute that the manifestation of the Christian faith in relation to same sex unions is '*discriminatory*' and contrary to the legitimate objectives of a public body. Further, I wish to dispute that such religious views are equivalent to a person who is, genuinely, a homophobe and disreputable ... In my view, the highest development of human spirituality is acceptance of Christ as saviour and adherence to Christian values. This cannot be seen by the Courts of this land as comparable to the base and ignorant behaviour. My heart is in anguish at the spiritual state of this country ... I am concerned that judges are unaware of these basic issues on the Christian faith ... I appeal to the Lord Chief Justice to establish a specialist Panel of Judges designated to hear cases engaging religious rights. Such Judges should have a proven sensitivity and understanding of religious issues and I would be supportive of Judges of all faiths and denominations being allocated to such a Panel. The Judges engaged in the cases listed above should recuse themselves from further adjudication on such matters as they have made clear their lack of knowledge about the Christian faith.

In his response, Lord Justice Laws said that Lord Carey misunderstood both the law and the role of judges in applying it. The law on discrimination is concerned with outcomes, not motives: whether or not the claimants' religious faith amounts to homophobia does not come into it. But this explanation of the legal position does not answer the "deeper concerns expressed in Lord Carey's statement and in Mr Diamond's argument" and Lord Justice Laws went on to tackle the wider issues:

> The common law and ECHR Article 9 offer vigorous protection of the Christian's right (and every other person's right) to hold and express his or her beliefs. And so they should. By contrast they do not, and should not, offer any protection whatever of the substance or content of those beliefs on the ground only that they are based on religious precepts ... the conferment of any legal protection or preference upon a particular substantive moral position on the ground only that it is espoused by the adherents of a particular faith, however long its tradition, however rich its culture, is deeply unprincipled ... The precepts of any one religion – any belief system – cannot, by force of their religious origins, sound any louder in the general law than the precepts of any other. If they did, those out in the cold would be less than citizens; and our constitution would be on the way to a theocracy ... The law of a theocracy is dictated without option to the people, not made by their judges and governments. The individual conscience is free to accept such dictated law; but the State, if its people are to be free, has the burdensome duty of thinking for itself.[74]

So according to Gary's legal team and a former Archbishop of Canterbury, religious freedom requires that an action – even though it would otherwise be grounds for legal challenge – should be protected if it results from religious belief. One of the country's most senior judges describes this position as "deeply unprincipled" taking us "on the way to a theocracy" – meaning a society where the government rules directly on behalf of, and applying the laws of, God. A minority of judges of the European Court of Human Rights call for protection of conscience, which, though not in quite the same place as the kind of 'theocracy' feared by Lord Justice Laws, is visiting the same territory – actions would be protected if genuinely motivated by deeply held reservations. Another very senior judge, Lady Hale, expects this idea to be taken seriously. Does this mean *any* conscience, *any* motivation for deeply held beliefs? Or should it be limited to protection of the Christian faith – and if so, who will define the kind of Christianity that enjoys this legal privilege? Lord Carey's answer is for this to be a matter for the panel of 'religiously qualified judges' to determine.

Is Lord Justice Laws right about the road – to 'theocracy' – Lord Carey is trying to get us to travel? Under Islamic Shari'a law, cases are not determined according to a common public code applying equally

---

74 Court of Appeal judgment released 29th April 2010.

to all. Instead, 'religiously qualified judges' determine a Muslim's guilt and punishment in accordance with the orthodox interpretation of Scripture. Lord Carey's proposal sounds very much like a Christian version of Shari'a.

In the public eye
CC cases attract widespread publicity – especially in Britain in the *Daily Mail* and *Daily Telegraph*, but also in the mainstream BBC and independent broadcast outlets. Its cases are also widely carried on American Christian media where one broadcast reports a "new battle of Britain" in defence of Christian civilisation against a government "threatening to criminalise" Christian witness.

The success of this campaign is shown in the words of Os Guinness, who, citing the Eweida and Chaplin cases, writes:

> There are many oddities in the strict separationists' attempts to cleanse public life antiseptically of all religion. In England, elite calls for strict separation represent a de facto disestablishment of the Church of England before any legal disestablishment has been decided by Parliament or people – which is surely the only explanation of the Alice-in-Wonderland situation where a government department can ban the wearing of the cross in the workplace when the cross is the official symbol of the official church of the land.[75]

There was no 'government department' involved in these cases and no 'ban' on 'the wearing of the cross'. Nonetheless, Guinness, though an enthusiastic supporter of church independence, was persuaded that these disputes about jewellery in uniform codes – one in a private sector company and the other in a hospital – were about government "attempts to cleanse public life ... of all religion'" in order to disestablish the Church of England.

In 2009 Duke Amachree lost his job as a homelessness prevention officer for Wandsworth Borough Council. America's Christian World News Channel reported this as a case of persecution of Christians, suppression of free speech and democracy, and part of an anti-Christian tide of legislation in the UK, with an appeal from Andrea Minichiello Williams for churches to be allowed 'unashamedly' to share their faith. What actually happened was that Duke met a housing applicant who told him she had an incurable disease. Afterwards she made a written complaint to the council. The lady said that in a "half hour lecture" Duke had told her that her illness was a result of her lack of faith in God and that she needed to "find God". She asked for an apology and

75 Os Guinness, *The global public square: religious freedom and the making of a world safe for diversity,* IVP, Downers Grove, Illinois, 2013, p107.

action from the council to prevent him "doing the same to anyone else who might be more seriously offended or, worse still, be encouraged to ignore medical advice".[76] The council suspended Duke on full pay and advised him to get legal advice, with a warning that the matter should be kept confidential. Duke got legal advice from CC's Christian Legal Centre (CLC). At a formal hearing, Duke's CLC lawyer asked how far a worker should go in not mentioning God to clients – for instance, would it be acceptable to say 'God bless' when bidding farewell? The council representatives said it would be best to keep God out of discussion. CC then – before the council had reached a conclusion in Duke's case – issued a press release headed "CLC Case: say 'God bless' and we'll sack you" revealing details about the complaint under investigation. Andrea Minichiello Williams was quoted as saying

> We are supporting Mr Amachree in this case because it is absurd to think that any public body could be in a position to enforce a policy which means that you can't even say 'God Bless'. This would effectively mean that faith would become entirely privatised. A Christian cannot leave faith out of any aspect of his or her life including work.[77]

Duke was then dismissed for two breaches of his terms of employment: the inappropriate lecture to the client, and the breach of confidentiality in permitting the CC press release. Duke appealed to an employment tribunal which

> concluded that the decision to dismiss was within the range of reasonable responses. However, it stated that, if the misconduct had been limited to the inappropriate interview comments, it would have had some doubts as to whether or not those allegations alone were sufficient to justify dismissal. It might have been influenced by the lack of guidance given to Mr Amachree on what was appropriate 'small talk' during interviews. But the reality was (the tribunal found) that the decision was taken against the background of a serious breach of confidentiality, on which the council does have clear guidelines for staff.[78]

So in fact the council had no "policy which means that you can't even say 'God Bless'". There was, the Tribunal noticed, no such guidance, and this finding might have helped Duke save his job – had CC not decided, with Duke's consent, to make public a claim that it *was* council policy, in a release that broke confidentiality and fatally undermined Duke's credibility as an employee.

A CC case can appear in the media even before internal disciplinary proceedings begin. Colin Atkinson was an electrician working for

---

76 http://www.xperthr.co.uk/law-reports/in-the-employment-tribunals-december-2010/106429/#amachree
77 *Daily Telegraph,* 28 March 2009. www.telegraph.co.uk/news/religion/5066075/Council-worker-suspended-for-suggesting-terminally-ill-woman-put-her-faith-in-God..html
78 See footnote 76.

a housing association in Wakefield, Yorkshire. He was in the habit of placing an eight-inch long palm cross in the windscreen of his company van. There was a complaint (where from is disputed[79]), Colin rejected a request not to display his cross, and after lengthy discussions with his union representative, was summoned to a disciplinary hearing where he was supported by the union representative as well as the CC's Christian Legal Centre. Before this hearing, the *Mail on Sunday* ran a story saying that he was "facing the sack". The newspaper published photographs not of just Colin's work van, with the cross, but also an internal view of the office of Denis Doody, Colin's manager, showing a picture of the Marxist revolutionary Che Guevara fixed to the wall. The far right British National Party (BNP) held a demonstration in support of Colin. In the event Colin was not sacked, but was by now working as a trainer based in one depot, so no longer needed company transport. His use of the company van for his journey to work was withdrawn. In its list of cases, CC describes Colin as a "van driver".

Another CC case where the facts were not as claimed is that of Nohad Halawi. According to CC, Nohad was 'sacked from her job at London's Heathrow Airport after false rumours that she was "anti-Islam"'. In fact, Nohad had her own limited company which provided services to Caroline South Associates, which had a contract to provide staffing for Shiseido, a Japanese cosmetics company, which had a contract with World Duty Free to operate a counter at London Heathrow Airport. Nohad was free to accept or reject assignments at the counter, and to provide staff of her own choosing to cover these assignments. World Duty Free arranged for the airport operator to provide the airside pass needed to cross security lines and reach the counter. Nohad's personal airside pass was withdrawn in June 2011. With the support of CC's Christian Legal Centre, Nohad launched a case in the Employment Tribunal, subsequently appealed, claiming religious discrimination, but this relied on her claim that she was an employee of World Duty Free and/or of Caroline South Associates. The courts consistently found that she was not an employee of anyone other than her own company; so she had no rights (such as protection from dismissal) as well as no duties under employment law. Whether the airside pass was withdrawn because of religious discrimination, or for some other reason, was never put to the courts for consideration. But describing Nohad as "the worker at Heathrow airport who has been dismissed

---

79 The source of the complaint is variously reported as being a tenant (according to the BBC website), a manager with Marxist sympathies (according to Richard Littlejohn for the *Daily Mail*) or as being anonymous (according to the trade paper *Inside Housing*).

after it was claimed that she insulted some of her Muslim colleagues",
Andrea Minichiello Williams wrote:

> This case has huge significance for what it tells us about the creep of Islamic
> extremism ... it is vital that Nohad's case is heard and not dismissed on a tech-
> nicality. Let us pray that the Employment Tribunal sees this... This case must
> be heard, not only so that Nohad can be reinstated after her unfair dismissal,
> not only to highlight the threat of radical Islam at Heathrow airport, but also to
> bring an end to stifling political correctness in public discourse.
>
> Ultimately, this is the only way in which the spread of Islamic fundamentalism
> can be arrested in this country.[80]

The succession of court actions about her employment status were
reported by the *Daily Telegraph* (27th November 2011) and the *Daily
Mail* (12th April 2013) as being about religious discrimination. The
Daily Mail also reported a number of Nohad's inflammatory allega-
tions. These included claims that Muslim staff were distributing extremist leaflets in the airport, that they had applauded the bombing of
London and that they were allowed airside without security checks.[81]

Bottom of the pile? The Johns case

A pivotal case for CC, reported as a test case for Christian rights and
freedom of speech, concerned Eunice and Owen Johns. According to
national press reports they were barred from being foster carers because of their Christian views. Once again the truth is rather more
complicated.

Eunice and Owen Johns come originally from Jamaica and are members of a Pentecostal church. For a year in the early 1990s they did
short term foster care for Derbyshire County Council. In January 2007
they applied to Derby City Council to become foster carers once more.
There had been changes in the meantime. Under 2002 legislation and
related guidance, councils had to ensure "that children and young people, and their families, are provided with foster care services which
value diversity and promote equality" embracing "services which recognise and address her/his needs in terms of gender, ethnic origin,
language, culture, disability and sexuality". The council sent Jenny
Shaw, an independent social worker, to assess the Johns' suitability.
According to Jenny's notes, considered at a later court hearing, "both
Eunice and Owen expressed strong views on homosexuality, stating
that it is 'Against God's law and morals'," though Eunice said that these
views did not come about as a result of their Christian faith but rather

---

80 See Andrea Williams' blog on the Christian Concern website, 1st December 2011.
81 *Mail Online*, 13th April 2013.

52

from her upbringing. They said they would not feel able to support a young person who was confused about their sexuality, and Eunice said that she had felt uncomfortable visiting San Francisco with its many gay inhabitants. Jenny put four scenarios to the couple and asked how they could support the young person:

1. Someone who is confused about their sexuality and thinks they may be gay.

2. A young person who is being bullied in school regarding their sexual orientation.

3. A young person who bullies others regarding the above.

4. Someone in their care whose parents are gay.

On the first question, Owen said he would try to "gently turn" the young person. On the second, Eunice would advise the young person to ignore it. She did not know what she would do about the third one, and on the fourth one, she did not think this would make any difference to the care she would provide. As Jenny's report noted, "Eunice's response to these hypothetical situations was somewhat superficial, and ignored the impact that her strong beliefs on the issue could have on her work with young people". There were a number of other visits and discussions, with problems around attitudes on sexuality and availability to provide care when both were at church. A note of a meeting on 24th September again found the couple "unable to acknowledge that their very strong beliefs would be likely to impact" on the way they would meet the Fostering Standards concerning diversity and equality. Eunice responded that it seemed "they could not be foster-carers because they are Christians" – a position the council strongly denied, noting that many Christians are fosterers; indeed, other members of the Johns' own Pentecostal congregation were foster carers with the council. At a Panel hearing in November, Eunice said: "I cannot tell a child that it is ok to be homosexual ... there has got to be different ways of going through this without having to compromise my faith." The conclusion of the hearing was that the Johns were understood as withdrawing their application, and the council's fostering manager wrote to them to confirm this on 5th December. Two months later, on 5th February 2008, the Johns wrote to deny that they had withdrawn the application. CC had been involved from the very early days of the case, and now its side of the story started appearing in the national media. A series of letters to the council accused it of religious discrimination.

The council's position, one of the letters claimed, was that:

> Christians and other faith groups who hold the view that any sexual union out-side a marriage between a man and a woman is morally reprehensible are per-sons who are unfit to foster. In short you seem to be suggesting that Christians (such as us) can only adopt if we compromise our beliefs regarding sexual eth-ics.
>
> Furthermore you have declined to respond to our question regarding your at-titude towards the Christian faith. We interpret your failure to respond as a sign that you are not prepared to deny that you view those of us who hold the above views on sexual ethics are 'homophobic'.

The council commissioned another report from a different social worker, Lynda Williams. Investigation and preparation of the 48-page report took six months. The report concluded:

> Eunice and Owen are kind and hospitable people, who would always do their best to make a child welcome and comfortable. They would endeavour, I am sure, to respond sensitively to a child and would take their responsibilities as carers seriously. The possible shortfalls described in this report in relation to their potential as foster carers do not detract from the fact that they are well-meaning and caring people, who are clearly well-regarded by their family and friends.
>
> It is fair to say that I retain a number of reservations about their potential to meet the wide range of expectations we have of carers to fulfil this very de-manding and complex role and would struggle to recommend them for ap-proval as mainstream foster carers.
>
> Panel may wish to consider, however, whether as respite carers for a child matching a specific profile, where the demands and difficulties are likely to be less intense and the role more circumscribed, approval would be appropriate. The question to be considered is whether for a somewhat less challenging role we demand the same degree of demonstrable insight and skill as for full time carers.
>
> In addition Mr and Mrs Johns' views on same sex relationships, which are not in line with the current requirements of the National Standards, and which are not susceptible to change, will need to be considered when Panel reaches its conclusion.

So back to square one! The Panel next considered the Johns' case on 10th March 2009. Now the CLC lawyers came up with a new solution: not to make any decision on the Johns' case, but instead to go to court for 'declaratory relief', in other words, for a resolution of the principles on which the issue should be resolved. The council accepted this. Over a year then passed before the lawyers made the application for a court hearing. This application asked the court to consider the following question:

How is the Local Authority as a Fostering Agency required to balance the obligations owed under the Equality Act 2006 (not to directly or indirectly discriminate on the grounds of religion or belief), the obligations under the Equality Act (Sexual Orientation) Regulations 2007 (not to discriminate directly or indirectly based on sexual orientation), the Human Rights Act 1998, the National Minimum Standards for Fostering Services and Derby City Council's Fostering Policy when deciding whether to approve prospective foster carers as carers for its looked-after children. Within that balancing exercise does the Local Authority have a duty to treat the welfare of such looked-after children as its paramount consideration?

For 'declaratory relief' to be considered, the court needed this question refined into a statement that it could be asked to endorse. Eventually the Johns, through the CLC legal team, put the requested declaration as follows:

(a) Persons who adhere to a traditional code of sexual ethics, according to which any sexual union outside marriage (understood as a lifelong relationship of fidelity between a man and a woman) is morally undesirable, should not be considered unsuitable to be foster carers for this reason alone. This is a correct application of the National Minimum Standards 7 'Valuing Diversity'.

(b) Persons who attend Church services at a mainstream denomination are, in principle, suitable to be foster carers.

(c) It is unlawful for a Foster Service to ask potential foster carers their views on homosexuality absent the needs of a specific child.

(d) It is unlawful for a public authority to describe religious adherents who adhere to a code of moral sexual ethics namely that any sexual union outside marriage between a man and a woman in a lifetime relationship of fidelity is morally undesirable, as 'homophobic'.

During the hearing, the council formulated the declaration they sought as:

A fostering service provider may be acting lawfully if it decides not to approve a prospective foster carer who evinces antipathy, objection to, or disapproval of, homosexuality and same-sex relationships and an inability to respect, value and demonstrate positive attitudes towards homosexuality and same-sex relationships.

Two High Court judges heard the case on 1st November 2010.

Just before this hearing, the *Daily Mail* reported:

Gay rights laws are eroding Christianity and stifling free speech, Church of England bishops warned yesterday. Senior clerics, including former Archbishop of Canterbury Lord Carey, spoke out ahead of a High Court 'clash of rights' hearing over whether Christians are fit to foster or adopt children.

The test case starting today involves a couple who say they have been barred from fostering because they refuse to give up their religious belief that homosexuality is unacceptable.

Supporters hope their legal challenge will set a precedent for the rights of Christians to foster children without compromising their faith.

But senior bishops fear that if the ruling goes against them, it could have devastating consequences for those with religious beliefs.

Either way, they believe the case will determine whether Christians can continue to express their beliefs in this country.

In an open letter, they warned that Labour's equality laws put homosexual rights over those of others, "even though the Office for National Statistics has subsequently shown homosexuals to be just one in 66 of the population".

The letter is signed by Lord Carey, the Bishop of Winchester Rt Rev Michael Scott-Joynt, the Bishop of Chester Rt Rev Peter Forster, and Rt Rev Michael Nazir-Ali, the former Bishop of Rochester.

They wrote: "The High Court is to be asked to rule on whether Christians are 'fit people' to adopt or foster children – or whether they will be excluded, regardless of the needs of children, from doing so because of the requirements of homosexual rights."

The court's assessment of the case put before them by the CLC team led by Paul Diamond is devastating – not just in terms of its legal merits, but also of the lawyers' confusion over Christian and Muslim views of marriage. Lord Justice Munby and Mr Justice Beatson wrote in their judgement, published on 28th November 2011:

Mr Diamond lays much emphasis upon various arguments, many of them couched in extravagant rhetoric, which, to speak plainly, are for the greater part, in our judgment, simply wrong as to the factual premises on which they are based and at best tendentious in their analysis of the issues. We do not doubt the sincerity of the claimants' views – both their views on the issues which underlie this litigation and their views as to the issues raised in the wider public debate which Mr Diamond seeks to canvass on their behalf – but as articulated by Mr Diamond they have little to do with the legal issues which are, alone, our concern.

Thus Mr Diamond's skeleton argument opens with these words, "This case raises profound issues on the question of religious freedom and whether Christians (or Jews and Muslims) can partake in the grant of 'benefits' by the State, or whether they have a *second class* status" (emphasis in original). He continues, "The advancement of same sex rights is beginning to be seen as a threat to religious liberty". He asserts that "something is very wrong with the legal, moral and ethical compass of our country" and that "Gay rights advocates construe religious protection down to vanishing point". He submits that the State "should not use its coercive powers to de-legitimise Christian belief". He asserts that what he calls the modern British State is "ill suited to serve as an ethical authority" and complains that it "is seeking to force Christian believers *'into the closet'.*" He identifies the issue before the court as being "whether a Christian couple are *'fit and proper persons'* (Counsel's use of phrase) to foster (and, by implication, to adopt) by reason of their faith" and "whether Christian (and Jewish and Muslim) views on sexual ethics are worthy of respect in a democratic society". The manner in which he chooses to frame the argument is further illustrated by his submissions that what is here being contended for is "a blanket denial on all prospective Christian foster parents in the United Kingdom", indeed "a blanket ban against all persons of faith", an "irrebutable[82] presumption that no Christian (or faith adherent) can provide a suitable home to a child in need of a temporary placement", that "the denial of State benefits to those who believe homosexuality is a 'sin' must be premised on the basis that such beliefs are contrary to established public policy" and that what is being said amounts to this, that "the majority of world religions [are] deemed to have a belief system that could be described as *bigotry* or *discriminatory* because of a code of sexual ethics that some people disagree with".

It is hard to know where to start with this travesty of the reality. All we can do is to state, with all the power at our command, that the views that Mr Diamond seeks to impute to others have no part in the thinking of either the defendant or the court. We are simply not here concerned with the grant or denial of State 'benefits' to the claimants. No one is asserting that Christians (or, for that matter, Jews or Muslims) are not 'fit and proper' persons to foster or adopt. No one is contending for a blanket ban. No one is seeking to de-legitimise Christianity or any other faith or belief. No one is seeking to force Christians or adherents of other faiths into the closet. No one is asserting that the claimants are bigots. No one is seeking to give Christians, Jews or Muslims or, indeed, peoples of any faith, a second class status. On the contrary, it is fundamental to our law, to our polity and to our way of life, that *everyone* is equal: equal before the law and equal as a human being endowed with reason and entitled to dignity and respect.

We add this. On these issues Mr Diamond seeks to equiperate[83] the views of Christians, Jews and Muslims. Thus he says (we quote his skeleton argument) that "all of the major religions (Judaism, Christianity and Islam) teach against homosexual conduct". He says, quoting the claimants' grounds, that "major faith groups (including Christianity, Judaism and Islam), hold to the orthodox view that any sexual union outside marriage between one man and one woman is morally undesirable", describing marriage for this purpose in his proposed declaration as "a lifelong relationship of fidelity between a man and a woman". We find these propositions surprising ... the Christian concept ... that marriage is "the voluntary union for life of one man and one woman, to the exclusion of all others", hardly accords with the *Sharia*, which permits a man to have up to four wives and to divorce any of them at any time by his unilateral pronouncement of a bare *talaq*.

Concluding, the judges said:

We have stated our misgivings about the exercise of the jurisdiction to consider whether to grant any (and if so what) declaratory relief. The defendant

---

82   Sic. Misspelling in original.
83   Sic. Misspelling of 'equiparate' in original.

has taken no decision and there is likely to be a broad range of factual contexts for reaching a particular decision, the legality of which will be highly fact-sensitive. Moreover, the parties have: (a) been unable to agree on an appropriately focused question for the court to address, (b) each identified questions that do not raise a question of law that can be answered with anything approaching a simple 'yes' or 'no', and (c) furnished the court with no evidence ... we have concluded that we should make no order.

By now almost five years had passed since the Johns' application to Derby city council, and over two years since the Christian Legal Centre proposed to settle the matter by means of seeking 'declaratory relief' from the courts. Nothing had been settled; the court said it could not possibly decide such an issue by means of broad declarations of legal principle, and it was for the authorities to make decisions based on the facts of particular cases.

The day after the judgment, a lengthy report appeared in the Daily Telegraph under the by-line Cassandra Jardine.[84] It quoted extensively from Andrea Williams and Eunice Johns, who, the report added, "is using the CLC's central London offices as a base". The report opened:

> Eunice Johns greets me, a total stranger, with an embrace. "I like to hug", she says. A minute later, when I am looking for a tissue to blow my nose, she hands me half her packet. These are the actions of a true Christian. And that's the problem. Eunice lives according to the instruction she finds in the Bible – and one of those instructions is that sex should be confined to marriage. For that reason, she and her equally beaming, gentle husband, Owen, have not been allowed to foster children.
>
> Yesterday, two High Court judges upheld the decision of Derby City Council not to approve the Johns family as carers. There were no objections to them saying grace before meals or taking foster children to church on Sunday. The sticking point was their answer to the question: "Would you tell a child it was OK to be homosexual?" The Johns replied that they would not. They would love a child regardless, but not endorse that lifestyle.

The Johns then returned to Jamaica where Eunice told the local press that she and her husband had been "told they can't foster" because "as Christians they don't believe homosexuality is right" adding:

> These people (gays) have more rights than Christians. We have been called retarded homophobics because we want to stand up for the truth

Andrea Williams visited Jamaica the following year and shared a platform with American organisations appealing to Jamaicans to keep the colonial-era 'anti buggery' laws. The news website Buzzfeed[85] reported:

---

84 A distinguished *Daily Telegraph* staff writer who, sadly, died of cancer a few months after this article was published.
85 Posted by Lester Feder on 8th December 2013. The reporter confirmed he was present when the remarks were made and his report was repeated by other sources including *The Independent* newspaper.

During her remarks, Andrea Minichiello Williams of the United Kingdom's Christian Concern said Jamaica had the opportunity to become a world leader by fending off foreign pressure to decriminalise same-sex intercourse.

"Might it be that Jamaica says to the United States of America, says to Europe, 'Enough! You cannot come in and attack our families. We will not accept aid or promotion tied to an agenda that is against God and destroys our families,'" she said, adding to applause, "If you win here, you will have an impact in the Caribbean and an impact across the globe"...

Andrea went on to share her views of the causes of homosexuality. She referred to Tom Daley, a sportsman who had recently announced that he was in a gay relationship: this, Andrea said, was a result of the death of his father, helping prove that homosexuality was 'not inborn'. The report continued:

Williams warned that removal of Britain's sodomy law was the start of a process that has led to more and more permissive laws, including equalising the age of consent laws for homosexual and heterosexual intercourse.

"Once you strip away all this stuff, what you get is no age consent ... nobody ever enforces that law any more."

In testimony recorded on the Christian Legal centre website, the Johns say the CLC lawyers:

have been with us from day one, and their support and expertise has been invaluable. We are so grateful that the Lord led us to them, because without their help, we certainly wouldn't have challenged Derby City Council's decision to halt our fostering application.

But in fact the Johns had not been 'barred from fostering' nor were judges asked to review such a decision. The matter was still under consideration when the CLC lawyers suggested taking the matter to the courts to seek a declaration. The lawyers then took over a year to make the promised application – eventually, this application happened within a day of Mr Justice Laws' consideration of the MacFarlane case and of Lord Carey's demand for senior judges to give way to a religiously qualified panel. The wording of the declaration when finally drafted was much too broad to allow a specific examination of the merits of the Johns' case. No one related to the Johns' case is recorded as branding them 'homophobic' let alone 'retarded', but this language corresponds to Lord Carey's rage against equality legislation and the judges who watch over it: as equating Christians with those are "disreputable ... base and ignorant". Taking the Johns case to court did not, and could not, do anything to decide their acceptability as carers. The claim of 'senior bishops' that the case would (as the Daily Mail reported) "determine whether Christians can continue to express their beliefs in this country" was plainly ludicrous. Nor was there need to ask judges, as Lord Carey and the other 'senior bishops' claimed,

> to rule on whether Christians are "fit people" to adopt or foster children – or whether they will be excluded ... from doing so because of the requirements of homosexual rights

CC and the *Daily Mail* (though perhaps not the Johns themselves) knew that there was no such exclusion. Derby always insisted that other Christians were fostering, as were other members of the Johns' own congregation. In another case, Vince Matherick and his wife were regular foster carers for Somerset county council. In 2007, a social worker called and asked questions similar to those being put to the Johns. Vince, who like his wife was among the ministers of the charismatic congregation at South Chard church, lost his temper ("I have to admit I lost my cool, and we had quite a heated debate with our social worker" he told Helen Weathers of the *Daily Mail*), announced his 'retirement' from fostering and drove a child in his care to another home, an event promptly reported by the *Daily Mail*[86] and the *Daily Telegraph*.[87] Somerset social services denied the claim by the religious correspondent of the *Daily Telegraph* that the Mathericks were "forced to give up being foster parents". The head of Somerset children's services told the BBC:

> No children have been removed from them because of an issue relating to equalities and there are no plans to remove children for this reason. Mr and Mrs Matherick were concerned that they might be expected to promote homosexuality. This is not the expectation of Children's Social Care.

After a meeting with social services on 31st October 2007, the Mathericks, with CC support, continued to be approved as fosterers. Two weeks later, when Eunice and Owen Johns appeared at the Derby panel, they referred to the Matherick case, saying that Vince's foster child had been "removed from his care", insisted they were "not prepared to say it is ok to be homosexual" and said they did not "wish to go into this kind of debate".

The Christian Institute issued a statement on the Johns case noting that the "judgment does not ban Christians with orthodox beliefs on homosexual conduct from fostering children; local authorities are free to take on Christians as before". The statement also pointed out that the case had been brought with the support of CLC, an "entirely

---

86 http://www.dailymail.co.uk/femail/article-490040/The-foster-couple-quit-forced-promote-gay-rights.html
87 http://www.telegraph.co.uk/news/uknews/1567160/Christian-foster-parents-condemn-gay-laws.html

separate organisation" to the CI. So the CI distanced itself from the distorted claim, made by the bishops and the press, that the Johns case was about the rights of Christians generally to foster. It stresses that it is not associated with this tactic. Having made this clear, the CI's statement continues:

> As the judges pointed out, Parliament has enacted equality laws containing competing legal rights such as those based on sexual orientation and those based on religious beliefs. It is very clear that equality laws are leaving Christians at the bottom of the pile. The Christian Institute calls on Parliament to act urgently to protect the rights of Christians and sort out this obvious injustice.

But nowhere in the Johns judgment do the judges say they found 'competing legal rights' to consider. They made no comment on the Johns' beliefs other than to note that they were 'clearly worthy of respect.' The Johns' views on homosexuality as such were not a subject of consideration, though their response to the first of the hypothetical questions from the first social worker was 'revealing'.[88] The judges asked Mr Diamond to say if he was challenging the lawfulness of any of the legal and regulatory framework, policies or guidance used by Derby city council for considering fosterers (nine documents were submitted), and his answer was that he was not. The idea that competing rights were putting Christians at the 'bottom of the pile' would make sense if the issue had been some sort of general ban on Christians being fosterers – but as the CI itself pointed out, there was no such ban in place or contemplated. The court was asked to accept the premise of the action – that the 'legal rights' of Christians and gays are 'competing,' that there is a 'pile' where the court's job is to decide who is at the top and who at the bottom. The court adamantly rejected this analysis. They went at length into the role of the courts and of the state in a secular society, stressing that it is not for the courts to make judgements about the validity of religious views, but that – and here is the key point – "invocation of religious belief does not necessarily provide a defence to what is otherwise a valid claim".

Equal – or marginalised?

Does this mean that Christians can never use the courts to defend their rights? Of course not. Here is the CI's account of a case.

One day in 2010 a Police Community Service Officer in the north

---

88 Mr Johns later did "not remember" having told social workers he would "turn" the sexual preferences of a child in foster care, though the reporting social worker reconfirmed that he had said the words. Readers may find it even more alarming that a would-be paid carer of vulnerable children might advise a victim of homophobic bullying to "ignore" it and has no idea what to say to a perpetrator.

of England, Sam Adams, approached Dale McAlpine after hearing him preach the Christian gospel on the street in the town of Workington. Sam had not heard any mention of homosexuality; still he took it on himself to warn Dale that he would be arrested if he did raise that subject. Dale said that he sometimes did describe homosexual conduct as a sin. Shortly after, PC Craig Hynes arrived and arrested Dale under the Public Order Act. After nearly eight hours' detention the police let Dale go with a bail condition that he would not preach, even in his own church. The Christian Institute funded Dale's defence, he pleaded not guilty in the magistrate's court, and the case was dropped by prosecutors before coming to trial. Dale later accepted £7,000 plus costs from the police to settle his claim in a civil action for wrongful arrest and imprisonment and breach of his human rights. Before the prosecution was dropped, Peter Tatchell, a prominent gay rights activist known for aggressive hostility to Christian critics of homosexual equality, publicly described Dale's arrest as an attack on free speech. The Executive Director of the National Secular Society agreed and offered to appear as a witness in support of Dale in his civil action against the police.

In another case supported by the CI,[89] Adrian Smith, a housing manager, lost his job for the "gross misconduct" of using his personal Facebook page to oppose permitting civil partnership ceremonies in religious settings. He took his employer to court for breach of contract. In a comprehensive demolition of the employer's case, Mr Justice Briggs found in Adrian's favour. Paragraph 62 of the judgment includes this comment on the employer's fear that Adrian had put at risk the company's hard-won reputation for good practice in equality and diversity:

> I cannot envisage how any such loss of reputation would arise in the mind of any reasonable reader of Mr Smith's postings ... the encouragement of diversity in the recruitment of employees inevitably involves employing persons with widely different religious and political beliefs and views, some of which, however moderately expressed, may cause distress among the holders of deeply felt opposite views.[90]

Peter Tatchell welcomed the High Court ruling as:

> a victory for free speech and fair play... I am glad that my statement in support of Adrian was used in his legal case and that he has been vindicated.[91]

---

89 Though a delay in getting legal advice resulted in Adrian receiving much less compensation under law applying to breach of contract than he would have received in a timely submission to employment tribunal. Adrian however insisted that he was not concerned at the level of financial compensation.

90 https://www.judiciary.gov.uk/wp-content/uploads/JCO/Documents/Judgments/smith-v-trafford-housing-trust-16112012.pdf

91 http://www.pinknews.co.uk/2012/11/16/peter-tatchell-facebook-ruling-is-a-victory-for-free-speech/

So Christians' rights to free expression can be upheld by the courts, with support from those who profoundly disagree with what is being said – not by claiming special privilege, but seeking equality before the law. It is not a matter of who is at the top, or bottom, of any 'pile.' It is the basis of the law that all are equal – and all have an equal stake in its defence.

Might this be a better defence of legal liberty? Here is one reason why: a liberty that is granted to one section of the community on the basis of particular merit or privilege can be removed on the basis that the merit has gone elsewhere. Those who are disadvantaged under one regime will naturally resent that privilege and seek to have it overturned. Equal liberty for all gives everyone the same stake in its defence. If times of oppression return, the state may seek to limit freedoms – but it will have to convince or confront every part of society, since every section has an equal stake in the matter. It is in solidarity with others, including those who may be otherwise adamantly opposed to what we say, that each of us best defends our own liberty. Freedom is indivisible – yours and mine, theirs and ours, come to the same thing. This is the argument used by John F Kennedy, and rejected by Rick Santorum.[92]

Missing the point: Victoria goes public

As we have seen, reports of alleged persecution of Christians often publicise misleading accounts of the facts put to the courts. One result is that the Christian community is denied the opportunity to make a serious evaluation of real questions about their witness in stressful and demanding situations. Take the case of Victoria Wasteney. According to Christian Concern, in a claim repeated by the *Daily Telegraph*, a National Health Service trust suspended Victoria from work "for giving a book to a Muslim colleague".[93] According to Andrea Minichiello Williams the lessons of the case are that:

> Week by week Christians are marginalised, threatened, sidelined, sacked and disciplined simply for holding normal conversations about their faith which is held dear to them.

> The United Kingdom has a strong foundation rooted in Christianity which has brought us freedom and flourishing. The NHS and our Education System were started by Christians – motivated by their faith. Our legal system was founded on Christian values and yet we now see that it is one of the most liberal and anti-Christian legal systems in the Western world.

> We need a radical review of the balance of rights in this country which is

92 See chapter 1, pp16–17.
93 Christian concern press release, 7th April 2016; *Daily Telegraph*, same date.

skewed to favour religions and ideologies other than Christianity. This is ironic given that it is Christianity that has given our society freedom, tolerance and hospitality

The Employment Tribunal appeal recorded the facts as follows. Victoria is a senior manager responsible for Occupational Therapy in a secure mental health facility. After starting to attend meetings of a group in London called the Christian Revival Centre (CRC), she asked to arrange a Christian service on her work site. She got consent for a three-month pilot of a "broadly based ecumenical worship group meeting the needs of service users across a range of Christian denominations" to be run by CRC, overseen by the NHS trust. Once it started, staff raised concerns. The meetings included speaking in tongues and laying on of hands. Patients and staff escorts were pressured into participating in singing, jumping, waving their arms in the air and clapping. Patients were encouraged to give money to CRC and given 'homework' of encouraging others to join the group. Victoria involved herself in escort arrangements for a patient for whom she had no care responsibilities. The 'group' was not meeting the brief of serving the 'range' of Christian positions. The pilot ended and CRC refused to take part in something closer to 'broadly based' worship. Victoria got permission for CRC to issue a letter explaining why the service closed: what she then offered was a set of CRC packs with sweets and DVDs, which the trust declined to circulate. Following an inquiry, the trust decided that laying on of hands and speaking in tongues should not take place on its premises. Victoria accepted an internal report and received counselling and an informal warning for crossing professional boundaries and failing to take account of her conflict of interest as a CRC member.

Later a staff member made a formal complaint that Victoria's attention had damaged her health and ruined her first year of professional practice. She was of Birmingham Pakistani origin, in her first year of employment and first time away from home. From the evidence in the judgment, it seems she was open to discussion about faith and social issues but resisted invitations to attend CRC and made no Christian profession. When this Muslim junior worker was sick, Victoria performed 'laying on of hands' and dictated a prayer for her to recite including the words 'Jesus you are the son of God' to seek healing.

Victoria was suspended from work during an investigation of the complaint. The investigation and suspension took nine months, an unacceptably long period. She then returned to work with a first written warning to last for 12 months. During the investigation, Victoria accepted that she had once again crossed professional boundaries and that the laying on of hands was inappropriate. She apologised.

It is difficult to see that the employer was acting unreasonably in disciplining a senior manager who disregarded policy. The facts of the case were not in dispute – Victoria agreed that she had (perhaps unintentionally) ignored a policy that she had previously agreed. Was the Trust being unreasonable in prohibiting 'laying on of hands' in religious activity in its premises? Did she, as a senior officer in a sensitive role, show insufficient regard for professional boundaries in promoting not just her faith but also the interests of her own church, a fellowship of the distinctive kind called 'charismatic'? These are reasonable questions. The false claim that Victoria had been disciplined for 'giving a book' to a Muslim junior worker meant that genuinely interesting and challenging questions would not be discussed among Christians. Instead the editor of one Christian paper, reporting the Christian Concern version of the case, added that next the Queen's Christmas broadcast would be censored for religious content,[94] and then published a letter from a NHS worker regretting that, as he expected, he would be banned from giving Christian literature to colleagues.

A political point?

"Streams of cases are being brought to make a political point" – so said an Anglican Bishop, the Rt Rev Alan Wilson, in a radio documentary about some of the events described in this chapter.[95] Is this a fair accusation? And if so, what is the political point that is being made?

We have seen twelve cases where Christians have been supported by either the Christian Institute or Christian Concern – three being claims made against Christians by others, and nine being claims submitted to the courts by Christians.

In two cases – those of the street preacher Dale McAlpine and the housing manager Adrian Smith – the legal system upheld Christians' rights of free expression. Their actions did not limit the freedoms of others. The Christian claimants were supported by non-Christians who take the same view of free speech. Were these cases making a political point? If so, it was this: no one has the right to require Christians to stay silent about their views, even if unpopular and offensive to many. There is no such thing as a right not to be offended by politely expressed debate. In making this point, Christians can expect support from all those prepared to defend liberty and equality in a free soci-

---

94 *Evangelicals Now*, May 2016.
95 Evangelical Christians and equality, The Report, BBC Radio 4, 24 March 2011

ety, and such cases should be brought promptly with adequate legal advice.

The other ten cases are different. In four – council prayers, Johns' fostering, Victoria Wasteney's warning and Nohad Halawi's airside pass – CC or the CI gave to the public and the media an account of the situation which seemed at variance with the recorded facts, to make the question considered in public discussion different to the one put to the courts. In another, that of Duke Amachree, an answer to a question in an internal hearing was taken out of context and released to the press to suggest that the council had a policy which, in fact, it did not. The publicity by CC, with Duke's approval, breached confidentiality and damaged his case beyond repair: publicity, it seems, took priority over winning the claim. In all these, the main purpose of the strategy does appear to be to make a political point, regardless of what might be adjudged to be the facts under consideration. This political point is that the proper liberty of Christians is being violated in favour of the interests of other groups, and that the courts have a secular agenda that fails to give due protection to Christians.

That leaves five cases – two of double beds and three of employees – where the facts as shared in the media were correct. None had a realistic prospect of success. Mr and Mrs Bull knew that, in continuing their double-bed policy after the passage of the 2007 Sexual Orientation Regulations, they would break the law. They decided to proceed anyway, knowing they would be practicing illegal discrimination and were "likely to run into trouble".[96] Gary Macfarlane was sacked because his employer thought he was not telling the truth when he promised to do a job for which he'd accepted training. His argument in court – that his good reason for not doing the job was that it was against his faith – conceded that his employer was right to think he was being untruthful about his willingness to do it. Shirley Chaplin thought her wish to wear a cross overrode her employers' judgment of safe working. Lillian Ladele wanted to avoid certifying arrangements not in accordance with what she believed to be God's law, even though she was an employee of a registration service operating in accordance with civil law.

I do not questions the sincerity of the views of these people or the hurt felt by each of these in their struggles with conscience. Mrs Bull told a radio interviewer:

It wasn't the fact they were homosexual that was the problem. It's the act. And

---

96 See footnote 95.

that's the word used a lot in the courtroom. We didn't want that act taking place under our roof because in the Bible God insists that what happens under this roof, we have to answer for.[97]

It must be stressful for an hotelier to feel personally accountable to God for sexual activity in rooms contracted to visitors to use overnight. But even if this has a biblical basis, and even if there is a legal obligation on customers to submit to a host's interpretation of the Bible, having two beds in a room shared by two people makes no difference to their ability to do "that act" in the privacy of the room supplied. Gary said that helping gay couples was against his religion, but he was content to provide general counselling to same-sex couples and sought training specifically aimed at assisting clients' sex life. Shirley thought her religion required her to wear cross-shaped jewelry, but there is nothing in the Bible about wearing crosses. The Bible does, however, expect Christians to be submissive to employers even if their demands are onerous, so it seems.[98]

To require employers to arrange staff assignments in a way that meets the religious sensitivities of each employee would be extremely onerous. (Hypothetically for illustration, suppose a restaurant employee becomes a Muslim and asks not to serve pork or alcohol.) The argument developed by the Christian Legal Centre in the case of Gary Macfarlane is that the human right to express a religion means that any action according with a religious motivation must be protected – that, in Lord Justice Laws' words, a religious motivation is a defence against an otherwise valid claim. This could obviously lead to penalties for Christians, once employees and businesses are allowed to discriminate between customers and tasks on grounds of religion. Who would be allowed to practice this discrimination, and against whom?

One answer is that just certain kinds of religion should be protected in this way, specifically including the Christian religion as understood by these claimants. There is, as Bishop Wilson says, a political point being made here – and it is a different one from the straightforward equal right to liberty of expression successfully claimed by Dale McAlpine, the preacher, and Adrian Smith, the housing manager. The unsuccessful political claim, made in the other ten cases, is that 'equality law is marginalising Christians' so Christianity should be privileged in law, to give people the right to require others – including employers and customers – to adjust to their Christian values. This can only work if a version of Christianity is defined and privileged in law.

97 See footnote 95..
98 1 Peter 2.18.

This unavoidably amounts to a demand to restore a Christian state. As we saw in the first chapter, this is, it would appear, the aim of key thinkers associated with CC and the CI. They demand nothing less than a return to 'Christendom.'

So is there anything to learn from the history of the rise and fall of the Christian state? This is the question considered in the next chapter.

God requireth not a uniformity of religion to be enacted and enforced in any civil state; which enforced uniformity, sooner or later, is the greater occasion of civil war, ravishing of conscience, persecution of Jesus Christ in his servants, and of the hypocrisy and destruction of millions of souls

Roger Williams: The Bloudy Tenent of persecution

Chapter 3

The Bloudy Tenent

How the church began

The first people to be called 'Christians' were followers of Jesus in Antioch. Lying on the Mediterranean coast in modern Turkey, Antioch was the third greatest city of the Roman Empire. According to the New Testament book of Acts, persecution forced early Jesus followers out of Jerusalem. They spread out around the eastern Mediterranean and preached to their fellow-Jews. But in Antioch, they came across large numbers of non-Jews who "believed and turned to the Lord". So great was the demand that the first preachers on the scene sent for reinforcements. Paul and Barnabas spent a year teaching the new gathering. Later when they returned to Jerusalem, they carried with them money raised among the new followers ("each according to his ability") to relieve need in the Judean church.[99]

Maybe Antioch was where Paul first saw in action the vision of what the church could become – a new type of community, where there is "neither Greek nor Jew, male nor female, slave nor free":[100] one where all the world's ways of dividing human beings by social hierarchy, gender and race count for nothing. The church is, for Paul, the 'bride of Christ'.[101] The leadership and organisation of the church occupies a significant place in his writings. It was vital for him to establish a sound blueprint for the local assemblies, as explained in his letters to the churches. They should be able to decide for themselves who would lead them and who would join them as participating members. If people show a consistent disregard of Christian teaching, then they are excluded from participating in the local assembly. Only those who believe may take part in the shared meal called the 'communion,' 'Eucharist' or 'Lord's supper.' The sign of becoming a believer is baptism by being dipped in water. The local church, as a body, has the right and duty to make decisions based on these principles. Some people may, as a result, be excluded from the particular activities and connections that mark out the community of believers. But this does not mean that Christians separate themselves from the wider society which includes

---

99   Acts 11:19–30.
100   Galatians 3:28.
101   Ephesians 5:32.

Christians among many others – that would be absurd. Christians are part of that wider society – its neighbourhoods, its markets, its productive and community life.

There was no expectation that they should dominate or control this wider environment. When it comes to government, "the powers that be are ordained of God".[102] Christians have no mandate to change the political system. They generally do what the system expects of them. Among Jesus' most intimate followers there were arguments over who would have the leading positions in the Kingdom.[103] Jesus called them aside. His words to them, according to Matthew's gospel, were

> You know that the rulers of the Gentiles lord it over them, and their great men exercise authority over them. It is not this way among you, but whoever wishes to become great among you shall be your servant

So this is the picture of the Christian community in the New Testament. It consists of people who have made a choice to follow Jesus. They form their own local associations which they regulate themselves, including deciding who can and cannot join their number. They mix in the wider society and submit to its rules and governance – with exception made only to follow their duty to speak about what they find to be true about Christ. Their leaders do not claim positions of authority in the wider society on account of their Christian service.

This was the form the Christian community took as it spread around the Roman world in the first 250 years of its existence, up to the start of the fourth century. Local assemblies baptised new believers, taught and read the scriptures including the gospels and Paul's letters, and met frequently to worship and celebrate their faith. Its members held their own meetings and ceremonies but otherwise participated fully in the wider society. As Tertullian's *Apology* said, in words addressed to that wider society of unbelievers at the end of the second century

> We sail with you, we fight with you, we till the ground with you, and in like manner we unite with you in our trading.

With the spread of Christianity

> the common cry is, the city is infested, town and country overrun with Christians. And this universal revolt in all ages, sexes and qualities is lamented as a public loss.

So the rise of Christianity was a "revolt" and a "public loss". It was generally accepted that to be a Christian was illegal; but in the early days of its growth, followers of the new faith, though living a life of

---

102 Romans 13.1.
103 Luke 9; Matthew 25

some uncertainty, could be left alone by the State.[104] In the year 64 AD, the emperor Nero put the Christians of Rome to terror and torture, but this was an exceptional event – blamed for starting a destructive fire in the city in order to clear space for a favoured building project, Nero used the Christians in the city as a handy scapegoat. For two hundred years there was no formal imperial policy to purge the state of Christians. Things were left to the discretion of provincial governors, often reacting to reports and accusations made in local communities. Fifty or so years after Nero's fire, Pliny the Younger was governing an area on the Black Sea coast of what is now Turkey. He wrote to Emperor Trajan seeking policy guidance on what to do about Christians. In his letter, he explains that he has been executing Christians if they refuse, on the third time of asking, to pray to the Roman gods, worship Trajan and curse Christ. Trajan's reply is that Pliny should not actively seek Christians to prosecute, but deal with accusations as they come in, provided they are not anonymous. Confessing Christians are to be punished, but those who recant may be pardoned. Later, in 180 AD, 12 Christian villagers, probably local peasants, were beheaded in Carthage, a major Roman-Greek cultural and commercial centre on the coast of what is now Tunisia in north Africa: they were, according to Tertullian, the first Christians in Africa to be put to death for their faith. When Cyprian, the bishop of Carthage, met a similar fate in 258 AD, he was the first African bishop to die in this way. The villagers in 180 AD were told to "swear by the genius of our lord the emperor and make offerings for his safety". Refusing, they said they would be loyal to the emperor, give "honour to Caesar as Caesar", keep the law and pay taxes, but recognise as God only the "king of kings and emperor of all mankind". They quoted Paul's letter to Timothy, had books and Paul's letters with them, and shouted out that they persisted in being Christian. Sentencing Cyprian in 258, the proconsul Galerias Maximus told him:

> You have long lived an irreligious life, and have drawn together a number of men bound by an unlawful association, and professed yourself an open enemy to the gods and religion of Rome

Cyprian would now suffer execution as an "example to those whom you have wickedly associated with you".

So to refuse to conform to the religion of the Roman state was to be 'irreligious'. In 249, the emperor Decius issued an edict that all sub-

---

104 Timothy David Barnes, *Tertullian: a historical and literary study,* OUP, Oxford, 1985, p.103. The following account of the early church under Rome also draws on: J. N. Hillgarth (ed.), *Christianity and Paganism 350–750: the conversion of Western Europe,* University of Pennsylvania Press, Philadelphia, 1986; and Christoph Markscheis, *Between two worlds: structures of earliest Christianity,* SCM Press, London, 1999.

jects must take part in Roman worship and obtain a legal certificate confirming that they had done so. Formal persecution of Christians began a little later when Valerian ordered Christian clergy to sacrifice to Roman gods, and provided a range of penalties for Christian senators and senior imperial officials. In 303, Diocletian ordered that all Christians hand over their Scriptures to the authorities. Bishops who agreed to comply were branded as 'traditores' ('handovers'), the origin of the English word 'traitor'. By 311 the church in Carthage was split, with a rival Bishop from each faction.

Meanwhile, at the end of the third century, Constantius Chlorus, the Caesar (deputy emperor) of the empire in the west, was tolerant of Christianity and not enforcing penalties. His son, Constantine, followed this lead. On his father's death in 306, the army in northern England proclaimed Constantine emperor. His power spread east until he took control in Rome at his victory at the Battle of Milvian Bridge in 312 – the battle where he is supposed to have seen a vision of the cross and heard the prophecy that he would 'in this sign conquer.' The following year the Edict of Milan granted general freedom of worship and restored property confiscated from Christians during persecution. As emperor and a professing Christian, Constantine involved himself in internal church business. He settled the long-running 'handover' dispute in Carthage in favour of the *traditore* claimants, resulting in the dissenting Donatist tendency – demanding to know what business it was to the emperor to interfere in their affairs – becoming the most prominent church in Africa for several decades. Briefly Constantine was ready to support the distinguished bishop, the great Augustine of Hippo, and use force to suppress the Donatists, but drew back when his attention was diverted east to complete his conquest of the whole Roman Empire. Constantine continued to act as a sponsor and arbitrator in settling disputes over the official theology of the church. But his position remained one of freedom of subjects, Christian or otherwise, to worship as they chose.

The church as state religion

Christianity became the Empire's state religion with the Edict of Thessalonica in 380:

> It is our desire that all the various nations which are subject to our Clemency and Moderation, should continue to profess that religion which was delivered to the Romans by the divine Apostle Peter, as it has been preserved by faithful tradition, and which is now professed by the Pontiff Damasus and by Peter, Bishop of Alexandria, a man of apostolic holiness. According to the apostolic

teaching and the doctrine of the Gospel, let us believe in the one deity of the Father, the Son and the Holy Spirit, in equal majesty and in a holy Trinity. We authorize the followers of this law to assume the title of Catholic Christians; but as for the others, since, in our judgment they are foolish madmen, we decree that they shall be branded with the ignominious name of heretics, and shall not presume to give to their conventicles the name of churches. They will suffer in the first place the chastisement of the divine condemnation and in the second the punishment of our authority which in accordance with the will of Heaven we shall decide to inflict.

GIVEN IN THESSALONICA ON THE THIRD DAY FROM THE CALENDS OF MARCH, DURING THE FIFTH CONSULATE OF GRATIAN AUGUSTUS AND FIRST OF THEODOSIUS AUGUSTUS

After some brief last resistance from the forces of Roman tradition, the victory of Catholic Christianity was confirmed in ten years from 429 to 439, when about 150 laws were passed to define and enforce its supremacy. As a result, the church became wealthy, its clergy immune from secular law and taxes and made the "arbiters between central government and their locality".[105] Notably in 435:

All pagan temples shall be destroyed by the command of the magistrates, and shall be purified by the erection of the sign of the venerable Christian religion

with death as the penalty for anyone who "mocked this law".

Thus the church ceased to be a voluntary association of believers and began its life as a compulsory association of subjects. Baptism stopped being a public affirmation of an individual's faith: instead, infants were baptised shortly after birth. The reading and teaching of Scripture on any large scale fell into disuse. The Catholic church rose to reach its position of supreme power in the old western Roman empire. As one historian puts it:

the church was a compulsory society in precisely the same way as the modern state is a compulsory society ... the medieval church was a state. It had all the apparatus of the state: laws and law-courts, taxes and tax-collectors, a great administrative machine, power of life and death over the citizens of Christendom and their enemies within and without. It was the state at its highest power.[106]

But one of the things that defines the state is its claim to a 'monopoly of legitimate force' within the territory it claims to control. And in this respect the church was defective. To use force against subjects, the church needed to look to the local kings and princes. So the era of Catholic domination in the west was always marked by tension over who was really calling the shots – the Pope or the network of rulers, starting with the emperor over the German territories? The

---

105 Hillgarth, p45.
106 R W Southern, Western Society and the Church in the Middle Ages, Penguin, Harmondsworth, 1970, pp17–18.

Pope blessed and sanctified the rulers, and claimed legal supremacy over them. At the height of its power, roughly from 1050 to 1300, the Papacy created public law and controlled its own administrative and judicial system which was widely used to settle disputes. The church through its clergy provided the trained, literate elite vital to the orderly progress of government, commerce and industry.

> But of course the church was much more than the source of coercive power … It was the whole of human society subject to the will of God. It was the ark of salvation in a sea of destruction. How far there could be any rational social order outside the ark of the church was a disputed question, but at best it could only be very limited … So the church was not only *a* state, it was *the* state … Not only all political activity, but all learning and thought were functions of the church … in all its fullness it was the society of rational and redeemed mankind.[107]

A fundamental idea here was that the church had the power to grant salvation. This understanding enabled successive Popes to grant dispensations or 'indulgences', which relieved the receiver from the duties and penalties that attached to their sin. From 1095, Popes used indulgences to proclaim that Crusaders (invading Muslim territory to the east) would go straight to heaven on death. By 1150, a Pope hearing a divorce plea was so distressed that he offered an immediate deal to the aristocratic plaintiff – if he would take back his wife and remain faithful to her:

> She will bring you immunity for all the sins you have so far committed, and I shall be responsible for them on the Day of Judgment

By 1344 indulgences could be purchased for the reasonable sum of ten shillings by "knights, parish priests and townsfolk" in England. Over the next 150, years the scope of the bargain, available through lay middle-men, covered a whole range of exemptions from everyday risks, and travelling salespeople went from town to town with the offer.[108]

Such scandalous abuse triggered campaigns for reform. Reform movements had always existed, and sometimes prevailed, within the church. What became the Protestant Reformation started in demands that the church restrain corruption and abuse as exemplified in the sale of indulgences. But it progressed among Catholic clergy whose reading of the Bible showed them that salvation and redemption were not granted by priests or churches, but came through knowledge of Christ's love as revealed in the Scriptures. A renewed church would

---

107 Southern, p22.
108 Southern, pp136–9.

have at its centre the study of the Bible, translated into the language of local congregations and spread by the printing press. A printed edition of the original Greek text of the New Testament edited by the great Catholic scholar Erasmus appeared in 1516. Martin Luther's German translation of the New Testament appeared in 1522 – by which time, famous as the author of the *Ninety-Five Theses on the Power and Efficacy of Indulgences,* he had already been excommunicated from the Roman church.

Zurich in Switzerland was among the earliest jurisdictions to authorise a church reformed outside the Catholic system. After a series of debates in 1524, the Zurich council decided a dispute in favour of its local clergy led by Huldrych Zwingli. In reaching this judgment, the council rejected the authority of the Catholic Bishop on a range of matters including the observance of Lent, the Mass and tithing. But it still maintained that all infants should be baptised, and that it – the council – should determine the form of worship in the independent city-state that formed the Canton of Zurich. Some of Zwingli's supporters were shocked by his acceptance of the council's authority over the new church, and pressed for what they saw as the scriptural model, where churches baptise their own believing members and conduct their affairs without political interference.

Defying the wishes of the council and of Zwingli, a group met at a home in early 1525 and here, members baptised each other. Some of their number were expelled from Zurich, and spread their influence elsewhere in Switzerland, Germany and Austria. In 1526 the Zurich council made 'rebaptism' an offence punishable by death.

On 5th January, 1527, a prisoner arrived at a fishing station on the River Limmat on the edge of the city of Zurich in Switzerland. He was tied to a pole thrust under his bent knees and placed in a boat. After rowing out into the river, his captors turned him into the water and left him to drown. So ended the life of Felix Manz. Not yet thirty years old, he was the first martyr from what became known as the 'Anabaptist' (re-baptising) movement.

The free church and the Reformation
So, as soon as the Protestant movement emerged from the Reformation, it entered into sharp and often violent dispute about two linked questions: what is the church, and what is the state? For the mainstream reformers, the church included the whole of political society and it was appropriate for the state to endorse that church. For their Anabaptist

opponents, the church could only include converted believers, and it was not the business of the state to recognise it. This was an innovation with profound implications for the future not just of Christianity but of the state itself. What would this new church become? And where did this leave the relationship of Christians and the state?

In February 1527, followers of the new movement met in the Swiss town of Schleitheim and agreed on what distinguished their model of church practice. The seven articles of the Schleitheim confession were:

1. Baptism to be of believers only: infant baptism was "the chief abomination of the pope".

2. The Ban: the church can, after warning, excommunicate converted Christians who have fallen away

3. Breaking of Bread: the eucharist may be shared only by those "united beforehand by baptism in one body of Christ"

4. Separation from the Abomination: believers are to "withdraw from Babylon and the earthly Egypt" including "popish and antipopish churches, drinking houses and civil affairs"

5. Pastors in the Church: pastors are to be appointed, and if necessary removed and replaced, by the church. They are to be of impeccable reputation outside the church. Their role is "to read, to admonish and teach, to warn, to discipline, to ban in the church, to lead out in prayer for the advancement of all the brethren and sisters, to lift up the bread when it is to be broken, and in all things to see to the care of the body of Christ"

6. The Sword: Christians may not hold office as "government magistrates" since the state, and the ability to use force to settle disputes, is provided "outside the perfection of Christ".

7. The Oath: believers may not swear an Oath. (Oath-taking was a common device for subjects of the state to swear their loyalty.)

The Schleitheim Confession was soon widely published. Three months after it appeared, its main author, Michael Sattler, was executed by dismemberment and burning by authorities in Catholic Austria. In 1530 Martin Luther advocated the execution of Anabaptists. In 1534–1535 Anabaptists in Munster established a city-state which unsuccessfully resisted conquest by force: the excesses associated with Munster (including polygamy and cannibalism) gave justification to the general suppression of Anabaptism. In most of Europe, Anabaptists were executed or banished.

In 1536 Jean Calvin began his work in Geneva, working with William Farel on a plan for a common church where all citizens would subscribe to a single confession of faith, with forms of worship approved by the city council and universal baptism of infants. Forced out of Geneva by popular dissent, Calvin withdrew to Strasbourg and described the situation in Geneva:

> Brothels have been erected; the Catabaptists[109] have their meetings daily; masses are said far and wide. Things ... could not be worse

Recalled to Geneva in 1541, Calvin was able to develop his new church in the form that became known as 'Presbyterian' where elders or 'presbyters' govern each church, overseen by regional and national layers of authority. He instigated the imprisonment, torture and banishment of Anabaptists. He was associated with only one execution, burning Servetus for the blasphemy of denying the Trinity. However Calvin did expel Anabaptists on pain of death, and since the fate of Anabaptists in most of Europe was to be executed, expulsion was tantamount to a death sentence.

In England, King Henry VIII completed England's break with Rome in 1536. But there was a question over how far England would ally itself, theologically and politically, with the Protestant Reformation. As a by-product of negotiations with the German Lutheran powers, Henry received a stream of warnings of the dangers of Anabaptism. In September 1538 a private letter in German, translated by the Lutheran theologian Melanchthon for the benefit of the English court, showed English Anabaptism being "silently but widely propagated".[110] Lutheran rulers warned the King not to associate with the spreading Anabaptist menace. In October the King launched a commission against the Anabaptist and other potential deviations, and in November, Anabaptism in England was outlawed with adherents to be exiled.[111]

Across Europe, persecuted and banished, Anabaptists formed wandering communities seeking to settle where they might hope to be left in peace – as one group, the Mennonites, were able to do in Holland from 1537.

So from the outset of the Reformation, the Reformers sought to create churches embracing all citizens of the political unit under whose authority they fell, but faced dissent from groups who rejected both the Catholic and the Protestant versions of the church and attempted to set up churches on what they believed to be the New Testament model.

---

109 A variant of 'Anabaptist'.
110 *Letters and papers of Henry VIII, Foreign and Domestic*, vol 13 part 2, no 265, p105.
111 Anja-Leena Laitakari-Pyykko, *Philip Melanchthon's Influence on English theological thought during the early Reformation period*, University of Helsinki PhD 2013, pp393–5.

The mainstream Reformers had the same view of personal Christianity as the Anabaptists: only those relying on a personal faith in Jesus Christ are saved. But they rejected the Anabaptist account of the church as an exclusive community of believers. To do this, the mainstream Reformers needed to justify infant baptism, a socially inclusive church and a role for the state in enforcing true Christianity. To come to this position, Calvin agreed that in the New Testament, Christians are those who believe and are then baptised. But this, he said, represented the conversion of pagans who had first been instructed in the meaning of the sign of baptism. Infants from a churchgoing family have already received instruction and can therefore receive the sign even though they do not understand it. The church, he went on, is entitled to count among its number those who profess belief even though they never attend for worship: they "in a sense belong to it until they have been rejected by public judgment". The state has a duty to protect true religion even though it has no right to define it:

> Let no man be disturbed that I now commit to civil government the duty of rightly establishing religion, which I seem above to have put outside of human decision. For, when I approve of a civil administration that aims to prevent the true religion which is contained in God's law from being openly and with public sacrilege violated and defiled with impunity, I do not here, any more than before, allow men to make laws according to their own decision concerning religion and the worship of God.[112]

The circle was thus squared by giving a degree of recognition to a nominal Christianity that is inherited even though it is not professed or practised. The church, now deemed to include (admittedly only 'in a sense') the whole community then has the right to require the state to "prevent the true religion which is contained in God's law from being openly and with public sacrilege violated and defiled" – this religion necessarily being the one defined by the all-inclusive church. Calvin endorsed the model of the church contained in Matthew 18.20:

> Wherever we see the Word of God purely preached and heard, and the sacraments administered according to Christ's institution, there, it is not to be doubted, a church of God exists. For his promise cannot fail: "Wherever two or three are gathered in my name, there I am in the midst of them."

But then he followed Augustine, the scourge of the Donatists, in interpreting the parable of the wedding feast[113] as justifying the suppression of independent churches (described as 'hedge churches' since the extra guests were conscripted from the tracks outside the city).

---

112 John Calvin, *Institutes of the Christian Religion,* book IV, chapter 20, part 3.
113 Matthew chapter 22.

In the later years of the 16th century a group emerged in England known as Brownists after the founder, Robert Brown. Later known as Congregationalists, this group combined a Calvinist theology with a view of the church as consisting only of professing believers, each congregation having the right to appoint its own ministers. They also held that the state has the duty to protect, uphold and enforce true religion.[114] This position was exported to America with the puritan colonists after 1620, and became established in Massachusetts. For this to work, there must be some identity between political control of the state and membership of churches. In 1631 the general court (parliament) of Boston agreed that full citizenship rights be granted only to church members.[115] In 1636 it took power to approve churches. This was challenged by Baptists who rejected the state's right to dictate in matters of faith and religious conduct, and by residents deprived of full citizenship rights (including voting) by not belonging (voluntarily or otherwise) to a recognised church. It caused both public life and churches to fall into disrepute as it inevitably rewarded hypocrisy. To cope with the demands to award the rights of citizenship, churches were encouraged to admit to membership so-called 'half way believers' considered to benefit from an 'external covenant' with God even though they did not share in the internal 'covenant of grace'. In 1750 Jonathan Edwards, widely viewed in evangelical circles as among the greatest of American theologians, was expelled from his pulpit for refusing to accept "half way believers" and the "external covenant". Thus in Massachusetts, Calvinist theocracy reached the point where it collapsed under the weight of its own contradictions. The purified church and the theocratic state are an unsustainable combination. If the state is to control religion then it must contaminate the church; and if the church wants to remain pure then it must decide how to settle its relationship with the state.

The 1527 Schleitheim model seems to establish the church community as a self-governing, stateless society, where in "the perfection of Christ", order is imposed without the use of force. The state is not illegitimate but is needed only to deal with the affairs of the unsaved who cannot enter this perfection. Menno Simmons, founder of the Mennonites, taught submission to the state wherever conscience allowed. Mennonites in the Netherlands received exemption from the Oath and from military service, mostly in return for the payment of a

---

114 See the confession of 1596 on: http://www.reformedreader.org/ccc/atf.htm
115 Leo F. Solt, *Church and state in early modern England 1509–1640*, OUP, New York & Oxford, 1990, p191.

special poll tax.[116] Early in the 17th century a group of English Baptists settled and studied in Holland. In 1612 they produced a 100-point confession.[117] This recognised the legitimacy of the state and taught submission to it ("the office of the magistrate is a disposition or permissive ordinance of God for the good of mankind"). The state must not involve itself with religion – "the magistrate is not by virtue of his office to meddle with religion, or matters of conscience, to force and compel men to this or that form of religion or doctrine" but confine itself to "civil transgressions". However it forbade entry into state service as being incompatible with a personal Christian walk, requiring acts of violence which a Christian "cannot possibly do".

This group of English Baptists influenced Roger Williams, an Oxford-educated ordained Anglican minister who emigrated to Massachusetts in 1631, where he proclaimed himself a separatist and opponent of the Massachusetts theocracy, briefly declaring himself a Baptist for a short time from 1638 before distancing himself from any organised church. Williams is best known for founding the state of Rhode Island, considered the first state in the world to be based on a separation of church and state: civil rights in Rhode Island were open to those of any religious persuasion and the state's remit was restricted to civil matters. In the midst of the first English civil war Williams published a celebrated polemic attacking state control of religion:[118]

> God requireth not a uniformity of religion to be enacted and enforced in any civil state; which enforced uniformity, sooner or later, is the greater occasion of civil war, ravishing of conscience, persecution of Jesus Christ in his servants, and of the hypocrisy and destruction of millions of souls.[119]

Williams set out a vision for a society where all individuals would enjoy "soul liberty" and so churches could find their own way to purity in faith and worship. But if God gives no authority to the state to legislate in religious matters, this begs another question: where does the state's authority come from? Williams answered "that the sovereign, original, and foundation of civil power lies in the people". The quality of civil government does not depend on any religious position, either of the rulers or of the people whose consent authorises their power.

Parliament had Williams' book burnt by the public hangman.

---

116 J W Allen, *A History of Political Thought in the Sixteenth Century,* London, Methuen. 1960, p46.
117 http://www.reformedreader.org/ccc/acof1612.htm
118 Roger Williams' *The Bloudy Tenent of Persecution* was first published anonymously in London in 1644 in the form of an address to Parliament. The edition quoted here is Roger Williams, *The Bloudy Tenent of Persecution for Cause of Conscience Discussed and Mr Cotton's letter Examined and Answered*, reprinted with an introduction by the Hanserd Knollys society, London, 1846 (available online in a Google digitised edition). For a short introduction see John M Barry, 'Roger Williams' big idea', *Smithsonian* magazine, January 2012: http://www.smithsonianmag.com/history/god-government-and-roger-williams-big-idea-6291280/?no-ist.
119 Williams, *The Bloudy Tenent...*, p2.

However, such convictions took hold in the New Model Army led by Williams' friend and possibly distant relative, Oliver Cromwell. The prominent Puritan minister and army chaplain Richard Baxter of Kidderminster, shocked to hear of "swarms of Anabaptists in our armies" went to see for himself and found "a new face of things, which I never dreamed of ... Independency and Anabaptistry were most prevalent':

> their most frequent and vehement disputes were for liberty of conscience, as they called it; that is, that the civil magistrate had nothing to do to determine of anything in matters of religion by constraint or restraint, but every man might not only hold, but preach and do, in matters of religion what he pleased; that the civil magistrate hath nothing to do but with civil things, to keep the peace, and protect the churches' liberties.[120]

This was indeed a "new face of things" and deeply alarming to Baxter's tendency, the generally orthodox Puritans who dominated Parliament. The civil wars started in the King's projects to impose the Anglican system – with Bishops, Prayer Book and liturgy – on his three kingdoms. He found himself having to call Parliament to try to raise taxes to pay for the results of his failed invasion of Scotland, where the Presbyterians of the 'Covenant' would have nothing to do with bishops and liturgy. In England in 1640 the King required clergymen, teachers and others in the educated elite to conform in what became known as the 'Et cetera oath':

> that I do approve the doctrine, and discipline, or government established in the Church of England as containing all things necessary to salvation ... nor will I ever give my consent to alter the government of this Church by archbishops, bishops, deans, and archdeacons, &c., as it stands now established, and as by right it ought to stand

The Parliament of England and Wales, even if it agreed on nothing else, was not about to give any encouragement to a monarch claiming a divine right to impose High Church conformity. Its 1641 counter-oath required an oath to support:

> the true Reformed Protestant religion, expressed in the Doctrine of the Church of England, against all Popery and Popish Innovations

This was just a starting point in the struggle to define the replacement for medieval church-state absolutism.

Godliness, democracy and the struggle for liberty of conscience

---

120 In A S P Woodhouse, *Puritanism and Liberty, being the Army Debates* (1647–9) from the Clarke Manuscripts with Supplementary Documents, University of Chicago Press, 1938.

The Parliamentary opposition to the King fell roughly into four groups: the Presbyterians, the Erastians, the Independents, and the 'sects'. The largest block, the Presbyterians, were orthodox Calvinists seeking a purified but inclusive church promoted and protected by the state. Independents, successors of the Brownite Congregationalists, favoured self-governing churches composed of converted believers, supported by a state that would promote and defend the true Calvinist Reformed faith. To their 'left' the Separatist and Sectarian groups – including the growing Baptist and Quaker movements – inherited the mantle of Anabaptism, opposed to any state involvement in matters of faith: for some of these, this meant communities separating into called-out churches to await the imminent reign of Christ, while others saw the potential for the separation of church and state in a lasting settlement. Those dubbed Erastians believed that the state rather than the church should define and impose a common religion. Who called the shots in shifting coalitions depended more on the military than the political situation. The Parliamentary side faced a Royalist army with potential support from Catholic forces in Ireland and continental Europe, with the prospect of being executed for treason if parliament lost. As the parliamentary general the Earl of Manchester put it:

> We may beat the king 99 times, and yet he will be king still. If he beats us but once, we shall be hanged.

To bring a Scottish army into the war in 1643, Parliament signed up to the Solemn League and Covenant guaranteeing Presbyterian control of the future church in all three kingdoms, striving for:

> the preservation of the reformed religion in the Church of Scotland, in doctrine, worship, discipline and government, against our common enemies; the reformation of religion in the kingdoms of England and Ireland, in doctrine, worship, discipline and government, according to the Word of God, and the example of the best reformed Churches; and we shall endeavour to bring the Churches of God in the three kingdoms to the nearest conjunction and uniformity in religion, confession of faith, form of Church government, directory for worship and catechising, that we, and our posterity after us, may, as brethren, live in faith and love, and the Lord may delight to dwell in the midst of us.

> That we shall in like manner, without respect of persons, endeavour the extirpation of Popery, prelacy (that is, Church government by Archbishops, Bishops, their Chancellors and Commissaries, Deans, Deans and Chapters, Archdeacons, and all other ecclesiastical officers depending on that hierarchy)...

But later the generalship of Oliver Cromwell proved decisive, and from 1647 the Independents and the Anabaptist 'swarms' in the New Model Army grew in confidence and influence.

As Cromwell's army moved towards victory, the terms of a post war settlement were debated. In 1647 the Army high command, in its 'heads of proposals', included on religion:

> An Act to be passed to take away all coercive power, authority, and jurisdiction of Bishops and all other Ecclesiastical Officers whatsoever, extending to any civil penalties upon any: and to repeal all laws whereby the civil magistracy hath been, or is bound, upon any ecclesiastical censure to proceed (*ex officio*) unto any civil penalties against any persons so censured

and the repeal of all legislation:

> enjoining the use of the Book of Common Prayer, and imposing any penalties for neglect thereof; as also of all Acts or clauses of any Act, imposing any penalty for not coming to church, or for meetings elsewhere for prayer or other religious duties, exercises or ordinances, and some other provision to be made for discovering of Papists and Popish recusants, and for disabling of them, and of all Jesuits or priests from disturbing the State.

But as the wider army, including delegates (known as 'Agitators') from the regiments, came to debate the post war settlement, it developed a series of versions of the 'Agreement of the People' in favour of Parliaments elected on a popular franchise, the rule of law and equal access to justice. The first version, in October 1647 included this on religion:

> That matters of religion and the ways of God's worship are not at all entrusted by us to any human power, because therein we cannot remit or exceed a tittle of what our consciences dictate to be the mind of God without wilful sin: nevertheless the public way of instructing the nation (so it be not compulsive) is referred to their discretion.

The rejection of compulsion in religious matters was shocking to the Presbyterian tendency which had previously dominated the Parliamentary side. 42 Presbyterian-minded ministers and teachers in Lancashire proclaimed:

> we are here led to express with what astonishment and horror we are struck when we seriously weigh what endeavours are used for the establishing of an universal toleration of all the pernicious errors, blasphemous and heretical doctrines broached in these times, as if men would not sin fast enough except they were bidden; or as if God were not already enough dishonoured except the throne of iniquity were set up, framing mischief by a Law ... a toleration would be the putting of a sword into a madman's hand; a cup of poison into the hand of a child; a letting loose of madmen with fire-brands in their bands; an appointing a city of refuge in men's consciences for the devil to fly to; a laying of the stumbling block before the blind; a proclaiming liberty to the wolves to come into Christ's fold to prey upon his lambs; a toleration of soul-murder...[121]

---

121 Samuel Hibbert, John Palmer, William Robert Whatton, J Greswell, *History of the foundations in Manchester of Christs College, Cheethams College and the free grammar school*, 1830, p395.

Samuel Rutherford published *A free disputation against pretended liberty of conscience* addressed:

> TO THE Godly and impartial Reader:
>
> I offer (Worthy Reader) to your unpartiall and ingenuous censure these my ensuing thoughts against Liberty of conscience, from which way looking to me with a face of Atheism, I call the Adversaries, Libertines...

The Presbyterian majority in Parliament called on the King to save the nation from the "heretical democracy" advocated by the Army.[122] The King allied with the Scottish Covenanters to start the second Civil War, which ended in the summer of 1648 when Cromwell's army defeated the Royalist and Covenanting forces at Preston, cut off their retreat to Scotland and hunted the remnants down in the English Midlands. The victorious troops refined the terms of their proposed settlement so that the ninth article of 'Agreement of the people' late in 1648 read:

> Concerning religion, we agree as followeth: — I. It is intended that the Christian Religion be held forth and recommended as the public profession in this nation, which we desire may, by the grace of God, be reformed to the greatest purity in doctrine, worship and discipline, according to the Word of God; the instructing the people thereunto in a public way, so it be not compulsive; as also the maintaining of able teachers for that end, and for the confutation or discovering of heresy, error, and whatsoever is contrary to sound doctrine, is allowed to be provided for by our Representatives; the maintenance of which teachers may be out of a public treasury, and, we desire, not by tithes: provided, that Popery or Prelacy be not held forth as the public way or profession in this nation. 2. That, to the public profession so held forth, none be compelled by penalties or otherwise; but only may be endeavoured to be won by sound doctrine, and the example of a good conversation. 3. That such as profess faith in God by Jesus Christ, however differing in judgment from the doctrine, worship or discipline publicly held forth, as aforesaid, shall not be restrained from, but shall be protected in, the profession of their faith and exercise of religion ... Nevertheless, it is not intended to be hereby provided, that this liberty shall necessarily extend to Popery or Prelacy. 4. That all laws, ordinances, statutes, and clauses in any law, statute, or ordinance to the contrary of the liberty herein provided for, ... are hereby, repealed and made void.

After John Lilburne and a small group of 'Levellers' were sent to the Tower in 1649, they smuggled out a revised version of the Agreement of the People including this statement on religious liberty:

> That we do not inpower or entrust our said representatives to continue in force, or to make any Laws, Oaths, or Covenants, whereby to compel by penalties or otherwise any person to anything in or about matters of faith, Religion

---

122 Christopher Hill, *God's Englishman: Oliver Cromwell and the English Revolution*, Weidenfeld and Nicolson, London, 1970 p100.

or Gods worship or to restrain any person from the profession of his faith, or to exercise of Religion according to his Conscience, nothing having caused more distractions, and heart burnings in all ages, then persecution and molestation for matters of Conscience in and about Religion

These various statements identify the different tendencies in revolutionary thought. The army's leaders are determined that Anglicanism is not to be imposed, and Catholicism is to be excluded, but what beyond that? Wider debate leads to the conclusion that freedom of conscience in religion is the central principle, but there may be scope for the state to sponsor a favoured public faith. This develops into a role for the state in promoting and teaching a soundly biblical public faith, with freedom for Christians, but with a reservation around the rights of Anglicans and Catholics. The radicals, locked up in the Tower, would go further, and abolish any state interference in matters of faith. On the opposite flank, Presbyterians are horrified by the whole idea of giving "liberty to wolves" – the state must enforce true religion.

Viewing these debates through twenty-first century spectacles, it is not obvious what is at stake for these people. We tend to think debates among believers must be about 'religion'. But all these groups believe the same thing, more or less: that Christians are individuals saved or put right with God through personal faith, and that truth is found in the Bible comprising the Old and New Testaments. They all search their scriptures with diligence and passion. This is the generation that has grown up with the Authorised Version of the Bible, the new English translation published with state authority. They grapple with the implications of a startling historical shift – for a thousand years and more the masses in the European West have been told that they are born Christian, that their eternal destiny is negotiated for them by the church, and that they must rely on the church for the truth about Christianity. The state's primary role is to enforce the will of the church. Now they discover, in the New Testament, that each man or woman can access Christian truth directly and sort out their eternal destiny for themselves. Tyndale's prophecy – that one day any ploughboy would know more about God's word than the priests of the 1520s – has come true with shattering consequences. The church, as an institution, is no longer the mediator between man and God: this much is clear. 'Church' is now 'Ekklesia', the self-governing gathering of believers. But where does that leave the state? Wasn't public life still a quest for a godly nation? This the Presbyterians and Independents agreed. Oliver Cromwell "waited for the day to see union and right understanding between the godly people" including "Presbyterians, Independents, Anabaptists and all".[123] After Parliament was purged first of those reluctant to wage war against the King, then of those who resisted his execution, the remnant from 1649 was known as the 'Rump.' When in 1653 this 'Rump' moved towards new elections, Cromwell, with the army at his back, dismissed it. Instead of an elected assembly, Oliver Cromwell nominated the so-called 'Barebones Parliament.' He told this new gathering that they existed because the majority of the electorate was not yet "brought to own the interest of Jesus Christ".[124]

Jesus Christ is owned today by your call ... you are at the edge of the promises and prophecies

Oliver Cromwell set out to fulfil the promise of a purified state religion, with teams appointed to remove unsound clergy and test the suitability of new ones. Baptists, Independents and Presbyterians were among the 'triers' and 'ejectors' sent to reform the Parishes. Catholic and Anglican worship were (at least in principle) both banned, as was blasphemy, but otherwise Cromwell was committed to toleration. Independent churches kept their separate identity and he was frustrated at their mutual intolerance and reluctance to commit to a purified national church. The new nominated assembly focused on law reform and other concerns of the less comfortable sections of society, and was soon dismissed. Cromwell hoped to translate his huge power and prestige, conferred by God-given military triumphs, into godly rule over a sanctified people; and he was disappointed. A parliament elected on the old franchise would never agree to religious toleration, and he rejected the Levellers' plan for a new popular franchise with a vote for all adults excepting women, beggars, servants and active Royalists. So he was left with military dictatorship as the only way to deliver his project for a free, uncompelled, Bible-based public religion. After Oliver Cromwell died, Monarchy returned. After a few months of manoeuvring around an alliance of Anglicans and Presbyterians, King Charles II and his courtiers were strong enough to crush the Presbyterians and impose Anglican conformity in church and state.

Toleration returned to England in 1689, to be gradually strengthened over two centuries and never again seriously challenged, but in the system founded on the Established Anglican church with its liturgy and bishops. Western Europe generally followed a similar path – maintaining state-established churches, except for the disruption imposed

---

123 Blair Worden, *God's Instruments: Political conduct in the England of Oliver Cromwell*, OUP, Oxford, 2012, p72.
124 Blair Worden, *The Rump Parliament 1648–1653*, Cambridge University Press, Cambridge, 1977, p209.

by the French Revolution, through the nineteenth century, but accommodating growing pluralism and diversity.

America took a different path. The 1791 Bill of Rights banned any federal religious establishment. In 1802, President Thomas Jefferson described this as making a 'wall of separation' between church and state, picking up on language used by Roger Williams in 1644. Williams called for a 'wall or hedge' between the God-made garden of the church and the man-made wilderness of the state. Separation in the USA has been more of a hedge than a wall – growing over the years, not built all at once. As a federal arrangement it did not at first apply to the various states of the union, most of which had established churches up to the time of the Revolution. It is generally reckoned that the last formally recognised, state-supported church lost this status when Massachusetts disestablished in the 1830s. But remnants persisted. The state of New Hampshire barred non-Protestants from elected office until 1876.[125] As late as 1961, the US Supreme Court heard (and upheld) an appeal against Maryland's constitutional requirement preventing an atheist taking a public job.[126] In 1971, the Court heard a case organised by the American Civil Liberties Union (ACLU) in order to prevent state funding of religiously-based (mainly Catholic) schools. The Court found in favour of the ACLU claim, presented on its behalf in the name of a Mr Lemon. The resulting three-point 'Lemon test' bans state funding that advances or inhibits a religious cause, including funding for religious education in schools. This is a marked contrast with Britain or many European countries where state-funded religious education is widespread.

American Christianity flourished on its side of the 'hedge'. Between the Revolution and the Civil War, the Christian churches in the USA experienced extraordinary growth, almost entirely among the churches with no history of establishment – especially in Baptist and Methodist churches. These churches, says the historian Mark Noll, grew after:

> renouncing the traditional mechanisms by which Christian churches ... protected their social prerogatives and inculcated their traditions ... in place ... came informal, voluntary means of exerting social influence ... churches liberated from formal establishment ties ... were also liberated to construct a new nation

With a massive, pan-national social and economic presence, these independent, evangelical churches:

---

125 The constitution allowed only Protestants to be elected as legislators or as Governor.
126 In the case of Torcaso v Watkins.

stressed the need for moral choice, the capacity of redeemed individuals to create their own nurturing communities, and the image of human existence as a staging ground for personal and social transformation[127]

and this "played an extraordinarily significant part in making democracy work".

Thus the new USA worked out Roger Williams' vision – a society where 'soul liberty' for all means it is for churches to find their own way to purity in faith and worship; and where, in partnership with the freedom of the soul, the state is accountable to the people.

Setting the church free

On each side of the Atlantic, the aftermath of the Reformation saw political systems struggle to combine Christian churches based on New Testament principles – as voluntary gatherings of believers – with a state-promoted public Christianity. These aims proved incompatible. In Massachusetts the churches had to bend to democracy by admitting to membership those who were in truth indifferent to the faith. In England military rule was retained at the expense of returning to the path towards democracy, and in a few years both godly rule and democratic progress fell away.

England returned to the model of a national church which could live with – 'tolerate' – dissent while retaining its established place at the heart of a monarchical state. It would take another two centuries before the House of Commons was elected on something like a mass popular franchise. Could Oliver Cromwell have used the Army's moment of power to launch democracy in England two hundred years sooner? Perhaps he could. Instead he heard a different call – to unite the godly into a Christian elite backed by armed force, and try to sanctify an unwilling nation.

America took the other path. It separated church and state, and a Christianity founded on independent voluntary churches thrived at the heart not of the state, but of the wider society that drove the world's first mass democracy.

In both Britain and North America, Christians wrestled with the same problem and arrived, in different ways, at the same solution. The problem is: if we free the church to determine its own path, can we expect the state to hold and define a sound public faith? The answer arrives, in time and with experience, that we cannot. The fundamental problem is this: to maintain a distinctive public religion means there has to be some common identity between those who control the state

127 Mark Noll, *America's God, from Jonathan Edwards to Abraham Lincoln*, Oxford, OUP, 2002, pp175&197.

through political power, and those who teach and define the desired faith. In short, to fulfil the ideal of a pure public religion, the church must either hold political power, or submit to it. To establish a public faith must threaten the rights of churches to decide their own doctrines and membership.

Only if the state keeps out of matters of faith can the church be free. This insight, nurtured in Anabaptism, was the foundation for the 'hedge of separation' proposed by Roger Williams and celebrated by Thomas Jefferson. It has served American Christianity well.

But has the hedge now outgrown its welcome?

A new sacralism?

In an important book published in 1964,[128] the pastor, translator and historian Leonard Verduin saw Christianity in the USA having grown as the product of the free, uncompelled faith of the Anabaptist variety. This was what flourished under the First Amendment separation of church and state. Verduin used the word 'sacralism' to describe the rival version of Christianity, the state-sponsored public religion that earlier prevailed in both Catholic and Protestant states. Liberated from 'sacralism,' the churches, he claims, grew from representing 6% of Americans before the Revolution, to 60% when he wrote his book. In the twentieth century, according to Verduin, lingering 'Christian sacralism' – as advocated by such figures as the great Dutch pastor-politician Abraham Kuyper – was 'nostalgia' for the days of establishment.[129]

But in a postscript, Verduin warned of the threat of new versions of sacralism. He saw signs of the coming of a "new 'right' religion" – a "religiosity to which every right-thinking American would be expected to rally". In Supreme Court rulings on religious education, Verduin saw the First Amendment being interpreted to enforce "religious vacuity". Looking at these, Verduin feared 'a new sacralism, the sacralism of secularism'.[130]

In a few years the Religious Right arrived, defended by Francis Schaeffer in terms that Kuyper would have recognised: the state is provided by, and accountable to, God, with a duty to uphold true religion, though without prohibiting or imposing a religious belief on individuals. Then Father Neuhaus warned about the 'Naked Public Square'. Disliking the Religious Right, he hoped for a renewal of 'right' public religion in the American mainstream.

---

128 Leonard Verduin, *The Reformers and their Stepchildren*, Eerdmans, Grand Rapids, Michigan, 1964.
129 p.61.
130 pp278, 280.

The common good?

Looking back on this time, the philosopher Michael Sandel thought the liberal, secular politics of the 1970s failed to "connect with moral and spiritual yearning". Only the Religious Right met the desire for this sort of inspiration in politics. The state, for Sandel, cannot be neutral in matters of faith. He applauds Barack Obama for recognising this, and calls on others on the political centre and left to embrace a "politics of moral engagement". The Christian thinker Os Guinness places himself in the tradition of the advocates of church-state separation, but deplores "secularist strict separationism" and its "bid to exclude all religion from public life" making secularism itself a "new de facto establishment". Guinness calls for a "partnership between responsible religious and secularist leaders" to devise and enact "an agreed framework of what is understood and respected to be just and free for people ... and thus for the common good". In this "civil public square" based on an "agreed framework", citizens are to be "encouraged to be true to the faiths by which they live and yet taught to be civil to others and care to the common good of the society in which they live".[131]

In Britain, as part of a comprehensive position statement by the Fellowship of Independent Evangelical Churches (FIEC), the Oxford pastor Peter Comond cites Sandel and Guinness as witnesses in favour of the "civil public square" where there is "a clear division between church and state" and Christians "work faithfully for the common good".[132] In 2011, a network 'Together for the Common Good' (T4CG)[133] was established on the initiative of the daughter (a Catholic) of the late Anglican Bishop of Liverpool David Sheppard.[134] Drawing on the Sheppard legacy of Anglican and Catholic collaboration on social justice, the network has attracted an impressive range of contributors including independent evangelicals and non-Christians.

Separation of church and state: rediscovering Christian history

As we have seen in this chapter, separating church and state was proposed nearly 400 years ago, in the seventeenth century, by Christians wanting a church free of 'Christian' state control.

In the past, Christians have been familiar with the significance of this history. The great Christian politician Abraham Kuyper (prime

131 Os Guinness, *The global public square: religious freedom and the making of a world safe for diversity*, IVP, Downers Grove, Illinois, 2013, p186.
132 ed. John Stevens, *Independent church*, 10Publishing, Leyland, 2014, p113.
133 http://togetherforthecommongood.co.uk/
134 Sheppard is author of *Bias to the Poor*, Hodder & Stoughton, London, 1983. He was also a main contributor to the Church of England report *Faith in the City*, Church House Publishing, London,1985.

minister of the Netherlands early in the twentieth century) admired American separation, above all for its liberation of church and the spiritual life from state interference.[135] It was his model to take the Dutch Reformed Church out of state control and introduce 'pluriformity.' In this scheme, aspects of which remain to this day, the state does not favour any particular faith, but it does support various religious affiliations in education and other work for social well-being.

Today, however, church-state separation is understood differently, as a philosophy opposed to any Christian place in politics. The leading evangelical theologian Tom Wright thinks it came from the Enlightenment of the eighteenth century. It belonged, he says, to a movement to separate science (how we understand nature and society) from theology (how we understand God and the life of faith) – a movement that assumed:

> a split-level world in which 'religion' and 'faith' belong upstairs and 'society' and 'politics' belong downstairs. This assumption has effectively privatized religion and faith on the one hand, and on the other has emancipated politics from divine control or influence. God lives upstairs ... and doesn't bother about what goes on downstairs.[136]

The twentieth century journey from Abraham Kuyper's position to Professor Wright's took a line through the US Supreme Court's 1971 'Lemon test,' considered earlier.[137] This was when America's constitutional ban on religious establishment came to mean a bar against state support for education with a religious foundation. In contrast, many European states are prepared to respect a family's wish to include a religious context in state-funded education, even if politicians are not required to be prayerful believers in the way many American voters seem to expect.

For Kuyper, the purpose of separating church and state was to maintain, in modern conditions, a political order based on Christianity. Not everyone is a Christian; God's 'particular' or 'private' grace provides for some to be in his kingdom. Churches are associations of believers, beyond the proper power of the state to control. But there is, for Kuyper, 'common' or 'public' grace in God's provision for all humankind. State authority comes from God. Otherwise, he says, political authority is merely the rule of the strongest. Only because of God's mandate does a citizen feel constrained to submit to the state. This is why

---

135 Mark J Larson, *Abraham Kuyper, Conservatism and Church and state*, Wipf and Stock, Eugene, Oregon, 2015, pp37–38.
136 N T Wright, *God and Caesar, then and now: Festschrift for Dr Wesley Carr*, 2003: http://ntwrightpage.com/2016/05/07/god-and-caesar-then-and-now/. Professor Wright's ideas are presented in a number of books, including *God in Public: how the Bible speaks truth to power today*, SPCK, London, 2016, and in talks such as: http://youtube/rLiy-WlS9m
137 See p88.

the state must uphold true (i.e. Christian) religion. By this it resists an "attack on the foundations of public law". Denying the religious basis of political rule is to "affront the majesty of God as supreme ruler of the state".[138] This reasoning anticipates the thinking of the Religious Right, as expounded in Francis Schaeffer's *Christian Manifesto*.

Professor Wright does not acknowledge the Christian roots of separation, nor its part in strengthening both the church and the Christian foundations of political life. Rather, for him, it is a Christian retreat from political responsibility. Christ's call to join his kingdom is a call to establish "God's rule on earth, theocracy". Christians are called to practical politics in a 'cruciform theocracy' – rule shaped in, and by, the cross of Christ. 'Theocracy' in normal political speech suggests that God is understood to rule directly over the state, so when rulers act, they are simply transmitting God's will as vouchsafed to them. Professor Wright insists that this is not what he means. He understands 'theocracy' to mean God's ultimate control over all reality, which he thinks was denied by the Enlightenment doctrine of church-state separation.

As we have seen, it was Roger Williams and the Baptists, not enlightenment Deists a hundred years later, who were responsible for the innovation of separating church and state. Drawing on first-hand knowledge of Native American societies and comparing them with the theocracy of the Calvinist settlers with whom he had sailed west, Williams saw no superiority in Christian rule. The state did not need to be legitimised by formal acknowledgement of God's authority. It is the consent of the ruled, not the visible presence of the divine, that gives a state the right to expect submission.

Christians may reflect that – in line with New Testament teaching recorded in Paul's letter to the Roman church and Peter's to those in Asia – they do indeed submit to the state because it is God's will. That is one good reason to show consent. The non-Christian fellow-citizen may have a different reason, or none at all. The Christian submits because he or she knows it is God's will, not because the state says it is God's will. It would be perverse to withhold this consent on the grounds that the state does not publicly affirm what the Christian already knows.

Even so, the Religious Right wants to make Christians' consent to government conditional on a renewed Christian state. Christians ready to rediscover their history will see the flaws in this demand. The next, final, chapter explores the dangers of this moment and the alternative ways forward.

---

138 Abrahm Kuyper, *Lectures on Calvinism*, Eerdmans, Grand Rapids, Michigan, 1931, p103.

Secularism is Christianity's gift to the world

Larry Siedentop[139]

139 Larry Siedentop, *Inventing the Individual*, Allen Lane, Harmondsworth, 2014, p360.

Chapter 4

Uncommon good: Christians in the liberal state

Brexit with Bannon, and the defence of liberalism

Back in the summer of 2014, few saw significance in a political vision recorded on YouTube by Steve Bannon, a former naval officer turned Wall Street financier and media entrepreneur, in an address over Skype to the annual conference of the Dignitatis Humanae Institute (DHI). Even fewer foresaw Donald Trump becoming President of the USA in January 2017, with his campaign manager Steve Bannon by his side as White House chief strategist and Senior Counsellor.

In his talk to the DHI,[140] Steve Bannon describes the world as he sees it. We are at the start of a "brutal and bloody conflict" that threatens to destroy "everything bequeathed" to the West since pre-Christian times. To meet the crisis, the "church militant" must now unite and join in a "struggle against Islam" recalling wars between European and Muslim forces in the 8th and 16th centuries – struggles to which the Christian church owes its eminence. Having lost its 'Judaeo-Christian' foundation, the system based on liberal capitalism will fall in the face of challenge by the 'global tea-party movement',[141] including the United Kingdom Independence Party (UKIP) in Britain, the French National Front and comparable right-wing groupings in Germany, Italy and the Netherlands.

Knowing this worldview helps us understand the new turn in American politics, and explains the Trump team's fascination with Brexit and the British politician Nigel Farage. Here they find proof of the potential of the new global movement to deal a deathblow to the liberal, secular state. In its place will come a state fed on revived national and religious loyalties, drawing on racism which is "washed away" (Bannon's term) as the movement grows. The 'global tea party' seeks to re-sacralise the state, conferring power on the religious positions that it determines to privilege. To this end, it must overcome

---

140 Bannon spoke at Dignitatis Humanae Institute's 3rd annual conference taking place from 26th–29th June 2014 in the Vatican in Rome. His talk is on https://www.youtube.com/watch?v=FWXScQaZ2uI. A transcript is available on https://www.buzzfeed.com/lesterfeder/this-is-how-steve-bannon-sees-the-entire-world?utm_term=.prjY5O3N#.puGa8qNz
141 The Tea party is an American political movement claiming to be "a choir of voices declaring America must stand on the values which made us great". See http://www.teaparty.org.

resistance from Christians who understand the church to be a free association of believers, founded first on the New Testament and later on the liberal heritage from the Anabaptists, Roger Williams and the separation of church and state. In this effort to recapture the free church for the cause of political religion, it is aided by repeated but untrue claims that the secular state and legal system persecute Christians, by growing ignorance of the Christian roots of secular politics, and by anti-liberal attitudes spread from some political and philosophical sources.

The correct Christian position now, I propose, is in defence of a state that is liberal, properly secular and neutral in matters of faith. This is not to ignore some real challenges – to Christians engaged in democratic politics, to the family as a social institution, to liberty itself if the relationship of free church and secular state is not properly handled. Sometimes the Religious Right asks good questions, deserving a considered answer.

Here I will briefly examine some questions that my proposal raises. What defines liberalism? What is the state and how does it relate to society? Is there a danger of Christian 'extremism'? What is the political place of public Christianity?

Christianity and the priority of right

We have seen some Christians, rejecting the Religious Right, turn to another alternative to liberalism – the type of 'common good' argument especially associated with the public philosopher Michael Sandel. He criticises the liberal view of the state as set out in President Kennedy's famous defence of secularism[142] and in the work of his fellow Harvard professor John Rawls.[143] This liberal view is that

> government should be neutral on moral and religious questions, so that each individual could choose his or her own conception of the good life[144]

According to Professor Sandel this version of liberal theory triumphed fairly recently, having displaced an earlier idea – that 'liberty consists in sharing in self-government.' This earlier idea is 'not inconsistent' with liberalism but it does involve 'deliberating with fellow citizens about the common good'. This

> requires more than the capacity to choose one's ends and to respect others' rights ... It requires a knowledge of public affairs and also a sense of belong-

---

142 See chapter 1, p16.
143 Rawls' major works include *A Theory of Justice* (1971) and *Political Liberalism* (1993).
144 Michael Sandel, *Justice: what's the right thing to do?* Allen Lane, London, 2009, p246.

ing, a concern for the whole, a moral bond with the community whose fate is at stake

It needs 'certain qualities of character or civil virtues' and means that 'politics cannot be neutral toward the values and ends that citizens espouse.' Liberalism, according to Professor Sandel, fails to engage deep moral, religious and political commitments and excludes their adherents from public life. So the

> public philosophy by which we live cannot secure the freedom it promises, because it cannot inspire the sense of community and civic engagement that liberty requires.[145]

This critique has much in common with that of the Religious Right. Both hold liberalism responsible for a moral and spiritual vacuum at the heart of the state, so undermining the search for true freedom. The answer for the Religious Right is a Christian state; for the followers of Sandel, a new politics centred on deliberation over goodness.

What is at issue here? Both the Religious Right and the advocates of the common good say they agree with some of liberalism's tenets. That is to say, they agree that all are free to believe as they choose, to communicate what they wish and to come together to pursue any shared purpose. They agree that all human beings have equal moral worth and are therefore equally entitled to these general rights.

The disagreement arises over an idea called *the priority of the right over the good.* As Paul Rasor, with quotations from Michael Sandel, explains:

> The priority of right is a core principle of political liberalism. It is grounded in the liberal values of toleration and respect for the right of individuals and groups to choose their own ends. This commitment means that political liberalism seeks to articulate a basis for a political society that is "neutral with respect to ends", one, in other words, "that does not presuppose the superiority of one way of life over others". To do this, political liberalism distinguishes between the right and the good, or "between a framework of basic rights and liberties", on the one hand, and "the conceptions of the good that people may choose to pursue within the framework", on the other. The framework is constructed from basic principles of justice such as fairness and respect for equal rights and liberties, and it is in principle independent of any particular conception of the good life. The freedom to choose one's own ends is one of the rights protected by the framework.[146]

The priority of right does not mean that ideas about goodness do

---

145 Michael Sandel, *Democracy's Discontent*, Belknapp, Cambridge (Mass) and London, 1996, pp4–6.
146 Paul Rasor Theological and Political Liberalisms, *Journal of Law and Religion*, Vol. 24, No. 2 (2008–2009), pp433–462.

not matter, or that differences between such ideas are unimportant. It does not mean that there is no such thing as truth about what is good. It means that the pursuit of goodness is for individuals and groups, not to be a matter for politics and the state.

Understanding this was central to what Roger Williams achieved in the *Bloudy Tenent*. As we saw in chapter 3, Williams wrote to explain his dispute with the theocrats who controlled New England. He quotes his main opponent as saying that a good citizen, political leader or judge has to be someone of a sound religious position:

> A subject without godliness will not be bonus vir, a good man, and a magistrate, except he see godliness preserved, will not be bonus magistratus.

Williams answers that a good public official is like

> a good physician, a good lawyer, a good seaman, a good merchant, a good pilot for such or such a shore or harbour: that is, morally, civilly good, in their several civil respects and employments … A pagan or antichristian pilot may be as skilful to carry the ship to its desired port, as any Christian mariner or pilot in the world … A Christian pilot, he performs the same work, as likewise doth the metaphorical pilot in the ship of the commonweal, from a principle of knowledge and experience.[147]

The leadership of a state can be 'good' in the sense of 'civilly good' whatever the religious sensibilities that guide it. Like a pilot, a politician or official must "carry the ship to the desired port" – guide the state honestly and competently – not "command the souls" of citizens. Whether or not a Christian, any good pilot works on what Williams calls "a principle of knowledge". The difference is that a Christian "acts from a root of the fear of God and love to mankind in his whole course".

Before Roger Williams' breakthrough, Christians could not see their way round the problem of politics: either the state is a Christian institution, in which case Christians must fight over which form of Christianity is to rule; or the state is not a Christian institution, in which case Christians are to obey it where possible, but not participate in it. Williams solved this problem. The state can be run by anyone who is competent and honest, whatever they believe. The Christian enters public life not to make the state more Christian, but to give glory to God by doing the job well. The state is there not to uphold any particular version of goodness, but to protect the freedom of all to pursue goodness. It is an idea that translates into the shocking, revolutionary war-cry of Cromwell's Baptist and independent troopers: *the civil*

---

147 Roger Williams, *The Bloudy Tenent of Persecution for Cause of Conscience Discussed and Mr Cotton's letter Examined and Answered*: reprinted with an introduction by the Hanserd Knollys society, London, 1846, Ch XCI p.211.

magistrate shall have nothing to do in matters of religion.[148]

Professor Sandel thinks the principle of priority of right arose to allow for diverse opinions of goodness:

> Since people disagree about the best way to live, government should not affirm in law any particular vision of the good life. Instead, it should provide a framework of rights...[149]

In reading Williams, however, it is clear that political accommodation of diversity was not his main concern. He had no dispute with his opponents about the 'good life' – all were Bible-believing, Reformed Protestants. Williams objected to compulsion itself as the way to procure goodness. His reading of Scripture was that goodness could not be compelled. He saw that linking political power with church membership would corrupt the church and promote hypocrisy. He also found, especially from his close observation of New England's Native American neighbours, that people did not need to be Christians to govern themselves well. Established religion, he argued, was bad for goodness, and bad for good politics. From these insights he worked out the idea of separating church and state.

In any case, for the state not to affirm a particular religious or moral vision does not solve the problem of diversity. It can achieve this only if people accept that goodness does not need to be imposed or authorised by the state. If people do not accept this, then they must struggle for their own version of goodness to become the doctrine of government. So liberalism fails when introduced into societies where its values are not accepted. For liberalism to work, people must find within their own doctrines of goodness – religious or otherwise – that goodness is the fruit of voluntary reflection and action. It takes just a small minority to deny this – viewing the state as good only if it adopts a particular version of goodness – to disrupt, even destroy, a liberal state.

As we saw in chapter three, Roger Williams' concern was for "soul liberty". To support this liberty, he said, the state had to keep out of matters of religion. The state must not take a view on the truth of religious claims. A Christian believes that no one is good but God, so the search for goodness is a search for godliness, and the state does not come into the matter. The state is not good or bad – it is neutral. God gives no authority to the state to decide or judge in religious matters. Many think that doing God's will is what gives the state its right to demand obedience. For them, the priority of right raises a problem

---

148 See page 82.
149 Michael Sandel, *Democracy's discontent*, p 4.

– what gives the state its authority? Williams considered this and answered "that the sovereign, original, and foundation of civil power lies in the people". So for Roger Williams, self-government follows from finding that politics is *not* the search for goodness.

This fulfilled the quest for the freedom of the church that started in the Anabaptist revolt against the Protestant Reformation. Roger Williams made clear what would establish this liberty. If the church is to have its essential freedom of association, the state must not limit this freedom, which means the state is not entitled to say what is, and is not, the correct order and doctrine for the church. The state is not able to judge what is, and is not, Christian. It follows that the state cannot limit the freedom of anyone to associate and communicate whatever they wish – subject to any proper limitations to protect public safety. The basis of all this is what we now call the priority of the right over the good – the state cannot decide what is good; only individuals, and the groups they are part of, can do that.

The founding mind of liberalism is usually considered to have been that of John Locke. But half a century before Locke's *Treatises on Government*, Roger Williams established basic liberal principles in the *Bloudy Tenent*. Underpinning these is the priority of right. Christians should, therefore, be wary about attempts to draw them into the camp of the 'common good'. The priority of right is a hard-won Christian principle of government. It secures the liberty of the church, and through that, the liberty of all.

This is not well understood. Many British Christians have not even heard of Roger Williams. Many accept the conventional idea that liberal politics was the fruit of the Enlightenment in a reaction against conservative, bible-based religion.[150] Others find liberty's origin in Protestant penetration of the expansionist, English-speaking political establishment[151] that built the 'Anglosphere'.[152] Neither approach can credit the role played here of rigorous, biblical analysis of the relationship of church and state.

Michael Sandel suggests that priority of right liberalism is fairly new, having really started with court rulings in the 1940s, holding that

---

150 e.g. Paul Rasor, p434: "theological and political liberalism emerged largely as products of the Enlightenment".
151 For example, the Barnabas Fund, protesting against anti-Christian bias which it says forced the Conservative politician Andrea Leadsom out of the race with Theresa May to become UK Prime Minister in succession to David Cameron, writes: '[F]rom the sixteenth century onwards freedom of religion gradually developed into one of the UK's defining national values, something that also became true of other countries that emerged from it, such as the USA, Australia, Canada and New Zealand.' See: barnabasfund.org/news/Editorial-Barnabas-Fund-calls-for-a-national-conversation-about-anti-Christian-prejudice-and-bullying, 15th July 2016.
152 Dr Boot writing on the Christian Concern website, http://www.christianconcern.com/our-concerns/freedom-of-speech/the-criminalisation-of-christianity-and-the-destruction-of-civilisation, 16th October 2015.

the USA's constitutional ban on establishing religion prevented state funding of education with a religious basis.[153] According to Professor Sandel, this new liberalism crowded out an earlier model of a free society – one that fostered self-government through a common quest for goodness. He traces this model back to pre-Christian thinking, especially that of the ancient Greek scientist and philosopher Aristotle.

Introducing his study of Politics, Aristotle wrote:

> Since we see that every state is an association of some sort, and that every association is formed for the attainment of some good (for it is to obtain what appears to themselves to be good that men always act), it is clear, that while all associations aim at some good, that one which is the highest of all, and includes all, will aim at the highest good in the highest degree; and this is that which is called the State and the State-Association.[154]

This is surprisingly illogical. We can see that some people, voluntarily, form their own associations in order to do good – but it does not follow that if all people are part of one association, this must be to do the most good possible. Even so, many, including Professor Sandel, follow Aristotle's idea that free people do politics in order to pursue goodness. A just society, say Aristotle and Professor Sandel, is one that recognises 'virtues' to be accorded 'honor and reward'.[155]

The liberal alternative says it is for individuals and groups to decide what is virtuous, live out those truths, and promote them to others: the job of the state and the legal system is to enable this to happen. So when Adrian Smith[156] wrote on his Facebook page that same-sex partnership in a religious setting was an 'equality too far', he meant that the state could recognise such arrangements but faith communities could, and in his view should, refuse to hold celebrations. His Facebook 'friend' at work complained to their employer that this was 'homophobic'. She was being a sound follower of Sandel and Aristotle – the state's recognition defined the best that society honours, and by denying this, Adrian became less than a good citizen and should be banished from the circle of those considered virtuous. Peter Tatchell, much as he disagreed with Adrian's assessment of same-sex partnership, came to his defence – all may reach their own view of what is 'good', and people with the same view are entitled to come together around it.

But what about those on the Religious Right? Why are they so at-

153 See footnote 43 on p17.
154 *Aristotle's Politics*, translated by W E Bolland, Longman, Green, London, 1877, p109. Available on line at https://archive.org/stream/cu31924071172914#page/n7/mode/2up
155 *Justice*, p186.
156 See p62.

tached to the idea of a Christian state? To understand this, we need to examine what they think the state actually is.

State, law and civil society

The Christian Institute founder and trustee, the Rev David Holloway, defines the state as "human society united both geographically and under a system of enforceable rules and regulations". Dr Boot of Christian Concern expresses a similar idea when he says the state is "only a differentiated public – that's all it is". If the state is the whole of society, then by definition all other social groups – such as families, associations, firms, unions and churches – fall under its authority. There can be no independence of the 'rules and regulations' enforced by the state. This seems to take us into the realm of totalitarianism – the doctrine that makes the state the *totality* of society. Religious Right thinkers would protest that they are not totalitarians. They see the state as existing under God with a specific mandate. This mandate limits its authority. Authority also lies with the family, the church and perhaps other institutions and with individuals. Totalitarian rule results when the state is controlled by rebels against God, who do not recognise the limits on their power. The passing of 'Christendom' makes this an urgent threat to society and to the church. So the Religious Right calls the church to restore Christian rule in the state.

There is a problem here. The New Testament does not seem to support this call. According to Paul in Romans 13.1, Christians are to submit to the civil authorities. The Religious Right has an explanation for this. This follows Roussas Rushdoony in reading Romans 13 to mean that Paul is

> establishing civil government in God and God's authority. The necessary consequence of this is to require civil government to be faithful to the foundation of its authority. To separate delegated authority from the delegator, God, is impossible.[157]

So when Paul says that Christians should submit to the civil authorities, he is (in Rushdoony's assessment) actually saying that they should submit only insofar as these authorities carry out God's commands. But if this was what the New Testament writers meant to convey, why is there no suggestion there that Christians should seek to change the state? The Religious Right solves this problem in claiming that Christian rule in Rome from 380 AD made "God's kingdom ... visible". When Jesus said that his kingdom was not of this earth, he actu-

---

157 Rushdoony, *Christianity and the State*, Kindle ed, loc 2272.

ally meant not *yet:* "His words implied that *at some time in the future,* His kingdom would possess institutional power. He would then have his defenders." 380 AD was the fulfilment of this moment – after this moment, "Christ had visibly defeated Caesar".[158]

So the Religious Right interprets Romans 13 in the light of later history, to conclude that "as long as the state rejects Jesus Christ ... and refuses to live by the every word of God ... it is a lie".[159]

Since the American Revolution, many Christians have accepted the separation of church and state. For the Religious Right, this follows from the pietistic individualism of most independent, evangelical churches. The focus on the converted individual, saved by personal faith in Christ, has grown some churches at the expense of the wider social mission, which is to make the whole of society accountable to God through its governing institutions. This seems to ask the church to choose between two lies to tell. It can preach the gospel of personal salvation and submit to the 'lie' of a state which is separate from the church, or it can uphold a 'true' political order and accept a lie about who is, and is not, a Christian. There is a contradiction to be resolved here. We can resolve this if we understand what the state actually is.

The state is one particular type of social authority. It exists across a defined area, within borders along the edges of its territory. It claims the exclusive right to use force within its territory, so it is defined above all by its ability to project decisive force inside its borders. It claims to be able to prevent intrusion across its borders, so its ability to project force usually needs to extend beyond these. It claims that its authority extends over any who live, or come, within its land, and people cannot opt out of this relationship – it is compulsory. To manage threats beyond its borders, a state always needs relations with other states. A state does not exist alone but is part of a system of states.

States have not always existed everywhere. Human beings and their social organisations can, and do, get along without them. People may live in small groups, often based on extended family networks; they may live as nomads, travelling with livestock; they may form networks of hunters protecting temporary settlements where crops grow and children are born and protected; all these arrangements and many others are familiar, and they can exist without states. In the Old Testament the Hebrew people escaped the grip of a state, fled across

---

158 North and DeMar, *Christian Reconstruction: what it is, what it isn't,* Institute of Christian Economics, Tyler, Texas, 1991, p34. Italics in the original.
159 Rushdoony, *Christianity and the State,* Kindle edition, loc 2186.

its borders, lived as nomads and settled in tribal (extended family) groups, all before they developed a state. It is a mistake to describe the state as a 'creation ordinance' as if it has always existed, having a status like that of family.[160] Thriving human society always has family; it often has no state. People can, and do, have law without the state: the Old Testament law existed before there was a state. People form relationships, work together for some common purpose, trade, marry, raise families, keep rules and do all manner of things without recourse to states.

Having a state however, does confer some really useful advantages. States enforce law, offer protection against violence, and enable settled groups to form productive relationships on vastly larger scales than are possible in non-state arrangements. States force everyone to share the burdens of activities that are necessary for the well-being of all.

To perform well, states require high levels of consent and co-operation among populations, with political systems to win and keep this active consent. But states are often weak, usually dependent on some degree of support from other states, and sometimes fail altogether resulting in disaster as violence floods in to fill the space vacated. Where states lack consent from local populations, other violent movements may win sufficient consent to displace the official state, and internal warfare takes place. The process of an ancient Jewish state forming and then failing is described in the Old Testament book of Judges. Amid a sea of savage violence, Jotham, sole survivor of a massacre, gives a bleak prophecy to the clans butchering their neighbours for short term gain. The state they are seizing is not a fruit tree or a vineyard, he explains. It is a thornbush, there to give defence by using violence. It will succeed if given care and respect. But leave it unwatered and, like the thorn in the dry desert, it will burst into flames and destroy all it was grown to protect.[161]

In most states in history, religion has been the way to give the state the essential 'legitimacy.' Rulers are understood to be descended from gods and able to mediate with their godly ancestors to bring good harvests and protection against invasion. Change of regime is interpreted as a transfer of divine protection, when the 'mandate of heaven' passes to new hands. Rulers are, we saw in chapter one, "kinsmen of the gods". Rulers gain legitimacy through their connection with the forces that are thought to control the direction of history. They must be con-

---

160 Dr Boot says that 'God has established' four 'creational structures' to 'provide government and authority' – marriage, family, church and state ('Voting and the role of the state', published on line by the Ezra Institute, 2016).
161 Judges 9.7–21.

nected with 'some god' and not 'just the economy'.

Christianity rejected that account of the state. The early followers of Christ understood that they had a duty to obey the state because God's arrangements for the world gave legitimacy to civil authority. It was possible to be obedient both to Christ and to an ungodly state. The New Testament broke the link between politics and religion. The early church understood both that:

> it is a fundamental human right, a privilege of nature, that every man should worship according to his own convictions

and that as Christians they could love, honour and give due homage to the Emperor of Rome.[162]

So to summarise: states are useful but not essential to human existence. Christians are to respect them, but are not required to establish or to control them. States need careful maintenance by a consenting population, and their failure and collapse is dangerous.[163]

What about law? Do Christians have a duty to sponsor and enforce godly laws?

Jesus spoke to a culture where religious leaders were expected to be model observers of biblical law and to decide on its application in particular cases. He was often interrogated about law-keeping and law-enforcement. Most of the time he turned such questions back onto the enquirers and accusers, challenging them to explore their own thinking in the light of the principles underpinning law. So, confronted by witnesses who had, handily, caught a woman "in the very act" of adultery, he suggested that the accuser without sin should throw the first stone in the legal execution of the victim.[164] Asked to settle a family dispute, he wanted to know who had appointed him a judge in the matter.[165] Asked if a faithful Jew should pay taxes to Rome, he prompted an inspection of the (Roman) face on the coinage.[166] In the gospel passage known as the Sermon on the Mount, Matthew presents Jesus dealing with questions about his law-keeping. I have not come to change the law or make a new one, he says: rather I have come to complete and fulfil the law. And what does this mean? To do no murder means to live without hate – for anyone who has hated has, as far as God is concerned, done the act of murder. Likewise, to do no adultery means to live without lust.[167] As his ministry proceeds, Jesus builds

162 Tertullian's address To Scapula.
163 There are different evaluations of the state in current Christian thought. For a useful overview of various recent schools of 'political theology' see: Elizabeth Phillips *Political theology: a guide for the perplexed* T&T Clark, London & NY, 2012.
164 John 8:7.
165 Luke 12.14
166 Mark 12.14-17.
167 Matthew 5:21–28.

his account of what being a law-keeping believer is about. The law, he says, comes down to loving God and loving neighbours.[168] This does not easily produce rules of the kind that helps a court administer justice. Let us imagine that a judge in a murder trial says the whole roomful – prosecutors, witnesses, jury, police, warders, the judge herself – all hate so everyone is a murderer and no one is qualified to convict or punish the justly accused murderer. The judge would be a sound Christian but a poor lawyer. Rules remain needed. But rule-keeping is not the way to peace with God. As the psalmist puts it, the sacrifice loved by God is a contrite heart.[169]

The New Testament records Paul's letters to emergent local churches, answering questions that are sometimes about order, discipline and rule-making in these communities. Writing to the Christians of Corinth,[170] he recalls that he has told them to have nothing to do with people who openly reject Christian standards of behaviour. But he wants to clarify something, since they seem to have missed an obvious point. He didn't mean they should stop dealing with the people of the wider society – that would be ridiculous. He was talking about how to regulate participation in the church itself. He is told of scandals in their fellowship – a man sleeps with his father's wife, apparently something to boast about! Throw this man out of your church, Paul tells them. He hears they are taking their internal disputes to the public authorities. This, he says, is a disgrace. These are not issues for the courts and councils of the state. Since when did people who are unrepentant cheats, adulterers and abusers have any say in matters of God's kingdom? The church can and should judge and resolve these things for itself. The church has 'rules and regulations', but the most it can do to enforce them is to exclude people from membership. The state is something else – it has the power and exclusive right to apply force within its territory. In a society where religion legitimates political power, it might seem obvious to take internal problems of church order to the state authorities. But Paul says this is a mistake. Sort it out yourselves, he says: you are capable of this. The state authorities are not part of Christ's kingdom so are unqualified to judge and apply church discipline.

The state's ability to exercise force might be limited by the disobedience of its subjects, who may decide to use force themselves to resist its authority. But Paul also says this is not an option open to the church.

---

168 Matthew 22:40.
169 Psalm 51:17.
170 1 Corinthians 5&6.

Christians submit to the state which does not "bear the sword in vain" – it has the right to use force.

Put in modern terms, Paul is saying that the church is a voluntary association. It exists and operates independently of state control over its affairs and decisions. The state is, in the words of the political theorist Harold Laski, compulsory association – people belong to it by birth or residence, and do not have a choice. A voluntary association is different – people belong by choice, and the rules of the association provide the conditions of acceptance and membership.

The idea of voluntary association is one with huge implications for the development of modern democracy. It is the foundation of what is called 'civil society.' Many scholars, going back to Alexis de Tocqueville,[171] have found that civil society is what makes democracy work. Civil society, according to Professor Michael Walzer, is that "network" which forms an "uncoerced space" between state and market.[172] In this 'space' citizens act to hold to account the agencies of government and business that direct the powers of state and capital. Civil society relies on two of the key building blocks of liberalism:[173] freedom of association, which gives any group the right to work together through voluntary agreement, and the right to communicate. In modern political arrangements, civil society balances the power of the state and of big business.

People and societies have laws and rules. There are laws about food that people keep individually and groups may enforce on their members. There are laws that govern sports and games. There are rules that apply to voluntary groups, rules in schools, rules that families make up and try to impose. There are also laws that apply to states and that states enforce. Some, but certainly not all, laws are supposed to be enforced by the state, and in practice the state enforces some, but not all, of these.

The state is also subject to law. The rule of law means that actions of the state can be reviewed, and overturned, by law courts. So judges, courts, police forces and prosecutors have some independence of the state, even though they are also its officers. They must know what the laws are, and why. So must the wider society. The rule of law is a biblical principle and something carried forward in societies influenced by the Bible. But it does not follow that the civil law should enforce what

---

171 Alexis de Tocqueville, *Democracy in America*, originally published in parts in 1835 and 1840.
172 'The civil society argument', Gunnar Myrdal lecture, Stockholm, October 1990: http://agonzalez.web.wesleyan.edu/span252/bibliografia/Walzer_CivilSocietyArgument.pdf
173 For a full argument on the idea of civil society and its foundations in these rights, see Cohen and Arato, *Civil Society and Political Theory*, MIT Press, Cambridge, Massachusetts, 1992.

the Bible says. It is for individuals and communities to consider the scriptures and how to understand, apply and use them. The laws to be enforced by the state are determined by the political process, whereby people decide their conditions for consenting to state power. Civil society – through its rights and structures of communication and association – holds the state to account, spreads knowledge of what the law is and what the courts do, and constantly scrutinises their working.

For a Christian, "no one is good excepting God alone".[174] The church is a voluntary association seeking the good life of its members and neighbours – a goodness that can be found only in submission to God under the headship of Christ. The church does not, according to Paul, defer to the state in deciding what is good, though it does submit to its authority as the civil power. So a Christian does not share the Aristotelian idea of politics as the pursuit of the highest good.

State-enforced rules promote peaceful conduct, and instil confidence in the complex human relations that underpin a technically advanced society. State services enable people to enjoy longer, fuller lives. These can all be good for the quality of life and human happiness. But the state does not define what is good according the standards of Christianity or any other faith or ethic. What the state can do is create a peaceful order with rights and opportunities for citizens, within which citizens and communities may pursue their conception of goodness and the good life. The rights to communicate and to associate are fundamental to this. These enable 'civil society' to exist, and the state to be held to account.

'ISIS minus the beheadings': Goodness, extremism and violence

The state is the social institution with the right to use force on behalf of society as a whole. When used – and respected – properly, it serves all citizens by providing a framework for public order, external defence and the fair distribution of burdens. But when it loses legitimacy, the question arises of whether resistance is justified with violent disobedience and force. The more a political movement regards itself as doing 'good,' the more it will tend to consider the use of violence for its good purpose of changing the state.[175]

Lord Carey, the former Archbishop of Canterbury, warned the

---

174 Mark 10.18.
175 For example, the political movement Momentum is the support network for Jeremy Corbyn, leader of the UK Labour Party, who believes in a socialist system where "everybody cares for everybody" (*Daily Mirror* 25th July 2015). In August 2016, following debate, Momentum agreed a proposal to amend its code of ethics to remove the word "nonviolent" in its description of its means to promote "progressive political change" (*Guardian* 19th August 2016). It justified this on the basis of 'self defence'.

Appeal Court about the way the courts were failing to see the role of faith:

> This type of 'reasoning' is dangerous to the social order and represents clear animus to Christian beliefs. The fact that senior clerics of the Church of England and other faiths feel compelled to intervene directly in judicial decisions and cases is illuminative of a future civil unrest.

The United Kingdom Independence Party (UKIP) won four million votes in the 2015 British general election. In a 'Christian manifesto' it claimed to be the "only major political party in Britain that still cherishes our Judaeo-Christian heritage", and accused other parties of having "deliberately marginalised our nation's faith". UKIP promised a "muscular defence of our Christian heritage and our Christian Constitution".

Gerard Batten, a UKIP Member of the European Parliament, and Christian Concern co-operated in producing a "proposed charter of Muslim understanding" for Muslim scholars and leaders to sign, to prove their acceptance of democratic values.[176]

> Asked why Muslims have been singled out, rather than followers of other faiths, Batten said: "Christians aren't blowing people up at the moment, are they? Are there any bombs going off round the world claimed by Christian organisations? I don't think so".[177]

On this view, statements coming from a 'Christian' perspective are exempt from monitoring for potential 'extremism' because Christians are non-violent. The problem with this (even if true) is that when Christians deny the legitimacy of liberal, secular pluralism, they claim to speak for non-Christians wanting to live under the protection of a 'Christian' order. Leadership then passes to those ready to capture that support for their political projects. So an ultimately successful candidate for the US Presidency, Donald Trump, promised to ban Muslims from entering the country. He says he does not need Christ's forgiveness.[178] But he proclaims himself a 'Christian' and tells a 'Christian' audience that they and 250 million other American 'Christians' have become

> less and less and less powerful in terms of a religion, and in terms of a force... [when] I get elected president ... Christianity will have power ... you're going to have plenty of power.[179]

176 Available on http://gerardbattenmep.co.uk/wp-content/uploads/2015/02/muslim1.pdf and on the Christian Concern website. The author, Sam Solomon, is at the time of writing Christian Concern's consultant on Islamic Affairs.
177 4th February 2014, http://www.theguardian.com/politics/2014/feb/04/ukip-mep-gerard-batten-muslims-sign-charter-rejecting-violence.
178 Donald Trump does not need to ask God for forgiveness as he doesn't have anything to apologise for, he told an interviewer in January 2016. See: http://uk.businessinsider.com/trump-on-god-i-dont-like-to-have-to-ask-for-forgiveness-2016-1?r=US&IR=T
179 Speech in Sioux Center, Iowa, 23rd January 2016.

Frank Schaeffer, son of Francis Schaeffer, produced the series of films that had great influence in shaping the Religious Right in the 1970s and 1980s.[180] The younger Schaeffer now repents and says about the movement he helped to launch:

> Dad's followers were told that (1) force is a legitimate weapon to use against an evil government; (2) America was like Hitler's Germany – because of legal abortion and of the forcing of 'humanism' on the population – and thus intrinsically evil; and (3) whatever would have been the 'appropriate response' to stop Hitler was now appropriate to do here in America to stop our government, which Dad had just branded a "counterfeit state".

> Is it any wonder that the (mostly) evangelicals running the far-right Republican Party these days see themselves as the children of a revolution? This is ISIS minus the beheadings, but the vibe is the same. Shutting down the government was nothing to these people. They see our government as the enemy, and they are running it.[181]

Consider these two commentaries:

> The fall of Soviet communism weakened the western hard left and forced it to look for new allies in its fight against capitalism and Christianity. It has now developed links to radical Islamists ... they are united in their hatred for America.

> A movement to deny the large-scale and long-term crimes against humanity committed by Islam ... is led by Islamic apologists and Marxist academics, and followed by all the politicians, journalists and intellectuals who call themselves secularists.

The first is from a pamphlet from a prominent Christian charity, distributed free in many churches in the UK.[182] The second comes from the European Declaration of Independence manifesto released by Andrew Berwick, better known by his Norwegian name of Anders Breivik, before he murdered 77 people in Oslo and on the island of Utoya, in Norway, on 22nd July 2011.

The modern state is, according to Rushdoony, founded on an illegitimate 'polytheism'. Obeying the state is worship of 'Molech'. Ideas like this have a way of travelling, including into minds like Breivik's, vulnerable to the self-indulgent romance of gratuitous violence. Extremist political ideas are like a virus nurtured in a laboratory. Stored safely and well managed, they may do no harm. But transmitted to where defences are weak, they become dangerous to the whole body.

Salt and light: the Christian presence in secular politics today

180 *How should we then live?* (1976) and *Whatever happened to the human race?* (1979).

181 http://www.salon.com/2014/12/24/my_horrible_right_wing_past_confessions_of_a_one_time_religious_right_icon/

182 Patrick Sookhdeo, *Returning Britain to its Christian Path*, Barnabas Fund, Pewsey, Wilts, UK, 2010, p14. In November 2015, Sookhdeo left his senior position in the charity and the booklet is no longer offered by the Barnabas Fund, which is best known for its relief work on behalf of persecuted Christian minorities around the world. It continues to run a campaign to expose and resist "increasing intolerance of Christian belief and growing restrictions on what Christians can say in the public square" in the UK and other Western democracies.

This book submits that Christians should endorse, and support, a state that is properly secular and neutral in matters of faith: that is to say, a state that does not favour, or claim to reflect, any particular faith or religious practice. It is for individuals, and the communities they shape, to reach their own view as to what is good. This view follows logically from Christian thought (the theology of the New Testament as understood in mainstream Christian thinking) and Christian history (the struggle for liberty of conscience and the freedom to communicate and associate). The highest good, to the Christian, is not found in the political action that shapes the state and its purposes. The highest good is found in relationship with Christ and in the work he has commissioned his church to do. The point of the state is not to do this work, but to provide and defend the framework of liberty that enables the church to go about its business, alongside others. This liberty falls if it is not shared with all, on the basis of equality.

This account does not deny that Christians in liberal society may, and sometimes do, face discrimination and undue pressure to suppress the inclinations of their faith. The question is not whether such problems exist, but whether they are a necessary result of equality or whether they can be tackled within the framework of equality. It is a question of perspective. The correct foundation for Christian action, on this analysis, is to endorse and develop the liberal politics of secularism and equality.

Supporting and advocating a genuinely secular state means actively resisting any turn to secularism as a new public religion. As Pope Benedict XVI (Joseph Ratzinger) put it:

> In the name of tolerance, tolerance is being abolished; this is a real threat we face. The danger is that reason – so-called Western reason – claims that it has now really recognised what is right and thus makes a claim to totality that is inimical to freedom. I believe that we must very emphatically delineate this danger. No one is forced to be a Christian. But no one should be forced to live according to the 'new religion' as though it alone were definitive and obligatory for all mankind.[183]

A genuinely secular state defends the rights of all – individuals, families, groups and communities – to liberty of conscience and the pursuit of the 'good life'. No religion or moral framework can claim exemption from the law or from the obligation to respect the rights of others. There is no right not to be offended, though there is a right to be protected against threats of violence or undue aggression. Subject to these limitations, secularism should secure the freedom of all to

---

183 http://www.catholicherald.co.uk/commentandblogs/2013/02/15/the-holy-fathers-warnings-on-secularism-and-religious-liberty-are-borne-out-by-the-consequences-of-the-same-sex-marriage-bill/

pursue, enjoy and share their religious or other convictions. Christians should understand this, perhaps more clearly than others. It is essential that Christians be among those engaged in secular politics – not least to define and maintain a proper secularism as it adapts to meet ever-changing challenges.

But aren't Christians obliged to keep quiet about their faith? How is that compatible with the needed Christian presence? Supporters of Andrea Leadsom, the last of Theresa May's rivals to withdraw from the post-Brexit contest to succeed Prime Minister David Cameron, expressed dismay at perceived media hostility to her faith. One item of evidence came from an interview by the political editor of Channel 4 News, Gary Gibbon. He asked Ms Leadsom about her political and business record. Ten minutes into a long interview, he noted that, as well as being a contest between two women, this was also one between two professing Christians. Then he asked: "Do you ever feel that you've been spoken to directly by God?" Initially faltering, the politician replied:

> That question is not one that is for – you know – open laughing at and poking fun at. I can absolutely feel that that's what you would like to. So, I absolutely am a Christian and I am very proud of it. And it absolutely acts in the background in my desire to have a very honest campaign with high integrity and so on. But if you are asking me, am I going to be sort of saying 'oh God's told me to do this and do that' well of course that's not the case.[184]

Commentary noted that here was the "question that Tony Blair was most afraid of answering",[185] recalling the famous words of that Prime Minister's advisor Alistair Campbell: "We don't do God". These words were not saying that Mr Blair, a devout reader of the Bible and the Q'ran, did not 'do God'. They meant he was not to be heard talking about it. Mr Campbell said the words repeatedly, in interventions during an interview about the occupation of Iraq, in order to distract attention from his boss's religious motivations.[186]

In Britain, there is suspicion about faith in the public sphere, partly based on a fear of theocracy – that is to say, a suspicion of leaders who think they are taking personal instructions from God. Most rulers in history have based their authority on their divine descent and their access to privileged information from the sacred forces that govern human existence. But Christianity rejects this. Theocracy is idolatry.

So the question that Mr Gibbon put to Ms Leadsom – you say you

---

184 7th July 2016. https://youtu.be/Hv3jtI4tha0
185 https://www.totalpolitics.com/articles/news/andrea-leadsom-stumbles-over-question-whether-god-speaks-her
186 Blair's Big Gamble, Vanity Fair, June 2003

are a Christian: does that mean God will tell you how to exercise your power as Prime Minister? – is reasonable and necessary. A Christian politician will pray about their job, like anyone else: for example, that she might work conscientiously and with wisdom. But Christians are not to use legislation, manifestos and military intervention as ways to preach the gospel, nor claim or expect private instructions from God about a task in hand. A Christian with political power is accountable like anyone else, in accordance with known rules and the information generally available to guide public decisions – acting, as Roger Williams put it, out of "the principle of knowledge and experience".

Today's Christian minority has a distinct – and urgently needed – contribution to make to the political life of the community. Larry Siedentop argues that, in depicting each human being as equally accountable to God, Christianity was 'Inventing the Individual', so laying the basis for secular liberalism. But now, in "a strange and disturbing moment in Western history" there is a lack of "an adequate understating of the relationship between secularism and Christianity". This erodes civil society by reducing liberalism to the satisfaction of short-term wants.[187]

One of the pitfalls of liberal pluralism is that debate becomes nothing more than a clash of vested interests. Democracy is reduced to a competition to offer better rewards to particular parts of the population. Christians should bring something different into the public square – something like the mind of Gabriel Oak, the prayerful shepherd-hero in Thomas Hardy's *Far from the Madding Crowd*. He "meditatively looked upon the horizon of circumstances without any special regard to his own standpoint in the midst". There is space for this kind of presence as 'salt and light' in today's liberal, secular and plural democracy.

This presence needs to be one that proclaims the Christian roots of liberalism. It looks beyond the rival claims of self-interest. It measures the virtue of the state by how freely questions about goodness and faith are asked and answered in mutual respect. It warns that good government comes with responsibilities that are to be shared and understood. It challenges society to be greater than the sum of its parts.

It is the necessary political presence of mature, twenty-first century Christianity. It gives voice to a mind that is – to quote Tom Wright – 'cruciform.' It is a presence shaped in, and by, the cross of Christ.

187 Larry Siedentop, *Inventing the Individual*, Allen Lane, Harmondsworth, 2014, pp362–3.

Index

Lightning Source UK Ltd.
Milton Keynes UK
UKOW03f1124240417
299768UK00001B/447/P